PENGUIN BOOKS

Shares

Martin Hawes is New Zealand's most successful financial writer. A popular speaker at seminars and conferences, he also serves on the boards of several companies and has had a financial slot on television.

After a brief period teaching, Martin set up an importing and manufacturing company which he ran for 10 years. Martin has contributed to many publications and is a columnist with *Herald on Sunday*. He has also written for *Canvas*, *North & South* and the *Accountants Journal*. Along with his partner, Joan Baker, Martin offers wealth coaching to clients who are seeking financial freedom.

Author of the definitive best-seller, *Family Trusts*, Martin's other books include *5 Ways to Save More Money on Your Mortgage*, *8 Secrets of Investment Success*, *Successful Super*, *20 Good Summers* and *Letters to Aston*.

Martin lives in Queenstown and likes to climb mountains, run, ski and rock climb.

Martin can be contacted at martin@martinhawes.com

NOTICE OF INTEREST

At the time of writing, my family trust and I hold units in managed funds giving me a beneficial interest in most of the companies in the NZX50. I also hold shares directly and indirectly in a range of New Zealand and overseas companies.

None of these companies nor any others mentioned in the text are being recommended as shares to own. This book is meant to be of a general nature and companies that are mentioned are only given as examples to illustrate a point.

Shares

Seven Secrets of Making Money on the Sharemarket

Martin Hawes

PENGUIN BOOKS

PENGUIN BOOKS
Published by the Penguin Group
Penguin Group (NZ), 67 Apollo Drive, Rosedale,
North Shore 0632, New Zealand (a division of Pearson New Zealand Ltd)
Penguin Group (USA) Inc., 375 Hudson Street,
New York, New York 10014, USA
Penguin Group (Canada), 90 Eglinton Avenue East, Suite 700, Toronto,
Ontario, M4P 2Y3, Canada (a division of Pearson Penguin Canada Inc.)
Penguin Books Ltd, 80 Strand, London, WC2R 0RL, England
Penguin Ireland, 25 St Stephen's Green,
Dublin 2, Ireland (a division of Penguin Books Ltd)
Penguin Group (Australia), 250 Camberwell Road, Camberwell,
Victoria 3124, Australia (a division of Pearson Australia Group Pty Ltd)
Penguin Books India Pvt Ltd, 11, Community Centre,
Panchsheel Park, New Delhi – 110 017, India
Penguin Books (South Africa) (Pty) Ltd, 24 Sturdee Avenue,
Rosebank, Johannesburg 2196, South Africa

Penguin Books Ltd, Registered Offices: 80 Strand, London, WC2R 0RL, England

First published by Penguin Books (NZ) Ltd, 2001

This revised edition published by Penguin Group, 2010

Designed by Mary Egan
Typeset by Pindar NZ
Printed and bound in Australia by Griffin Press

ISBN 978 014 320407 7
A catalogue record for this book is available
from the National Library of New Zealand.

www.penguin.co.nz

FSC www.fsc.org
MIX
Paper from
responsible sources
FSC® C009448

CONTENTS

AUTHOR'S NOTE

In July 2007, I sold almost all of my shares. I was already nervous about the global economy and the state of the markets: in fact, in the last edition of this book in February 2007, I warned that share values were becoming overdone. However, by July 2007 I was quite concerned with the wild lending on residential property around the world, overheated sharemarket valuations and a consumer binge that had gone mad. All of this conspired to encourage me to sell nearly everything, which I completed by the end of 2007. This timing proved to be fairly accurate as the markets fell substantially quite soon after. Although I bought back into the markets in a small way in May 2009, I remain cautious and, at the time of writing, I am still not fully invested.

I am largely a buy and hold investor, looking for long-term returns rather than trading. Buy and hold investing is the most profitable strategy; however, I do not believe that this necessarily means that you need to hold all the way through major market dislocations as we saw in 2008/2009. The events of that period have resulted in market falls of approximately 50% (depending on which market you look at) and, quite clearly, it is better not to hold right through a time like this. There are times when the market inflates a bubble and there is no value to be had. This is the time to get out. I think bubbles are reasonably easy to spot: a bubble in my book is when there is very poor income compared to the value of an asset and when people start to justify such extraordinary valuations with statements like, 'this time is different'. Indeed, I think as soon as somebody says, 'this time is different', you should get out of the market. At such times, when values are unjustifiably high, even a buy and hold investor like me is better to get out and wait for sanity to return. In times of market boom, greed takes over and fear is ignored. In fact, I think a little bit of fear is a very good thing.

However, a lot of fear is not a good thing and, when it comes to shares, Kiwis regrettably feel a great deal of fear. I am sure that a lot of this fear comes from the sharemarket crash of 1987, which is still deeply engrained in the Kiwi psyche. Nearly every family had one or more people who were badly affected by the crash of 1987 and many families still have a patriarch or matriarch who gives dire warnings about the events of that time. This is a great shame as it drives too many people into residential property which, at many times (especially at the moment), offers very poor investment returns. In fact, while shares do show a lot of volatility and will always do so, conditions in terms of market regulation and company governance are much better than what they were 30 years ago.

It is surprising to me that many Kiwis shun shares, because we are not afraid of business. Kiwis go into business in big numbers and do so very easily: any half-decent business idea sees them hang out their shingle and set up on their own as quick as you can say 'I'll be my own boss'. In fact, the majority of Kiwis are very friendly towards business – especially small businesses – and yet they are fearful in the extreme of shares. This is all quite strange because owning shares is, in reality, owning a part (a share) of a business. We are not scared of owning a business – we do that all the time – but we are somehow very scared of owning a part of one.

I think we need to reframe our understanding and the language of the sharemarket so that we think of it much more as buying a small slice in a business, rather than some commodity called shares. Shares are volatile and we are right to have a little bit of fear of that volatility. However, the underlying asset which is owned – a business of some sort or other – does not have a value which is particularly volatile at all. The shares may be volatile because of the vagaries of the sharemarket, but the underlying business tends to hold its value reasonably well. Certainly, the shares in the business may rise and fall in the short term but, over the long term, good businesses hold their value very well.

The problem in my view is what Ben Graham called Mr Market. Mr Market gives a value for your slice of a business in real time all day every day. The sharemarket continually values the part of a business that you own and the fluctuations frighten a lot of people. In fact, I think many people are better off not to look at share process very often. In the short term, share valuations are driven by emotion – fear and greed – rather than analysis. Eventually shares always come back to the true value of the business that they represent, but those who follow share prices too closely can often be influenced negatively by the volatility.

At the time of writing, there is much discussion in government circles about changes to property taxation. This is mostly designed at encouraging Kiwis to invest less in residential property and more in 'productive parts of the economy'. Taxing residential property more will result in fewer Kiwis entering that investment medium. However, at the same time, I think it is important that there is good education for New Zealanders regarding alternative investments, particularly shares. Most importantly, perhaps, is the change of attitude from owning something called shares to owning a small slice of a business. I do not think it is enough to discourage people from buying property without helping them find an alternative medium for their investment capital. In this respect, I think the NZX should play a bigger role in financial education as well as Government.

The Great Recession of 2008/2009 and the resulting sharemarket crash will do the case for sharemarket investment no good. However, there have been, over the last decade or so, some fantastic opportunities, particularly in emerging markets. The growth in Asian economies and the great gains in commodity markets has been quite fantastic for those who can tolerate the volatility. The transformation of the economies of India and China, in particular, cannot be ignored by investors – it seems to me to be a major turning point in an historical sense. These booming economies can – and should – be profited from either by buying into companies that do business in these countries (I personally do this through managed funds) or by buying into mining shares, especially Australian ones, which provide the commodities that fuel these economies. There will continue to be ups and downs in these Asian markets, but it is very hard to see the growth of China and India stopping completely for any great length of time.

I love the sharemarket. I have been buying and selling shares for over 25 years and have seldom been uninvolved for any significant periods of time. I particularly love the New Zealand market – for all its faults – its size and lack of diversification – it does generate an ease and satisfaction which comes from long acquaintance with the companies that are listed on it. Throughout this book I have generally used examples of New Zealand companies. This is mostly because I am most familiar with New Zealand companies. I invest offshore mainly through managed funds, only a little through direct investment into individual companies. More and more, I believe that this is a good way for people to operate – offshore exposure through managed funds but some degree of direct investment in New Zealand. I believe it is New Zealand companies with which my readers are most familiar – I think using known New Zealand companies helps people understand the principles of investment, principles that in any case work throughout the world. I have also used New Zealand examples to show that there are, indeed, some good companies and opportunities here deserving of your investment funds.

This book aims to help you understand the moods of the market. Understanding what is happening means that you can manage it and profit from it. You manage people best if you understand them – so too with the sharemarket. This is an area where the New Zealand market has an advantage for Kiwis – we know it and know the companies, and can track them very easily. Having recently become a grandfather, I now spend a bit of time in Pumpkin Patch shops. I am especially delighted as a shareholder in that company when I see how busy they are!

There are four major themes to this book:

1) Shares are an essential part of any investment portfolio. If you are serious about saving an investment, you simply must own shares. Owning a part of a business is simply too good a way to make money to ignore.
2) You can be both an investor and a trader. A key section of this book is on planning, which shows why and how you can divide your available funds and do well from both. The key to being both a trader and an investor is to recognise that these activities are quite different and that you should allocate funds to each and keep them quite distinct.
3) You should keep focused on the idea that when you buy shares you are, in fact, buying a little part of a business. In the final analysis, regardless of the ups and downs of the sharemarket overall, it is the performance of that business that will dictate the value of your shares.
4) You can beat the market. The market overall may or may not be doing well, but you can, with some work, make whatever investments you like and outperform the average.

At the end of the day, how things turn out on the sharemarket is entirely up to you.

Martin Hawes
March 2010

PART 1

The Market

CHAPTER ONE

You must own shares

If you are an investor, you have to own some shares. No matter what you think of shares, the sharemarket, sharebrokers – you have to be in the market.

Shares are the only way you can participate as an investor in the money-making activity that is business. Shares are simply a means of owning a small part (a share) of a business. The sharemarket is the organised means of buying and selling those shares and, in spite of the sophisticated use of computers and the seemingly impenetrable jargon of the participants, works just like the market for cabbages, wool, fish or real estate.

> Shares are the only way you can participate as an investor in the money-making activity that is business.

THE FEAR OF SHARES

Many people are fearful of shares and the sharemarket. Some people see the sharemarket as a volatile, unpredictable beast with a mind of its own. Its behaviour, its ups and downs, seem entirely inexplicable – and the downs seem to come just as soon as they have bought in, the ups as soon as they have sold out. Of course, the sharemarket crash of 1987 and the major losses in most global markets with the dot-com crash in the early 2000s and then again in 2008/2009 have put many people off. The New

Zealand market was badly affected by the 1987 crash and has still not recovered its value over 20 years after the event. While the New Zealand market was far less affected than other markets around the world from the falls in 2001, we certainly had a bad time in the Great Recession of 2008–2009.

The fear that people feel keeps them from entering (or re-entering) the market. The fear may come largely from ignorance but is real enough to the potential investor. The sharemarket seems like a casino for the rich and many feel excluded from it.

SHAREBROKERS DON'T HELP

The sharebroking industry has done little to encourage small investors to invest. Sharebrokers themselves do hardly anything in terms of public education, and when they do speak in public it is in jargon that simply reinforces the potential investor's impression that the market is not for ordinary people but for those in the know. Sharebrokers may rail against people investing in property by buying a second house. However, it is the real estate industry that has gone out to the public and told its story and so encouraged investors into property. The real estate industry, through seminars, newsletters, magazines and one-on-one contact, has beaten the share industry all ends up for the hearts, minds and money of the investing public. The balance between property and shares may be about to tip in favour of shares, but that is because of proposed tax changes to property, not the sharebrokers' or the NZX's ability to tell its story.

And yet, the sharebrokers have a good story to tell, as this book will show. There is a long list of companies that have been very profitable for investors. Shares are a profitable investment, an essential investment. Shares are easy to buy, a liquid (easily sold) investment with generally good returns over long periods of time. Shares are tax efficient and, best of all, if you go about it properly, investing in shares is a lot of fun. Why the sharebroking industry cannot explain all this to the public is beyond me.

PROPERTY VERSUS SHARES VERSUS DEPOSITS

In spite of this, I do not buy into the argument about which is the better investment. In my view it is a seriously stupid argument; one carried on largely by vested interests.

There are only three investments that you can make (shares, property and interest-earning deposits) and each has its place for investors. Indeed, most investors will want all three of these investment types in some proportion or other. This is partly for diversification and partly because each of the three has a particular role in what it contributes to the investor's financial situation. While I could predict with some certainty that shares and property will over the long term give better returns than interest-earning deposits, deposits are still important for the stability that they give a portfolio and for their liquidity.

Property is certainly less volatile than shares, and ownership gives a sense of control. However, shares are more liquid and will probably give better long-term returns for investors. Each investment type has its own advantages and disadvantages:

Investment Comparison

	DEPOSITS	PROPERTY	SHARES
Likely returns	Low	Med	High
Volatility (risk)	Low	Med	High
Tax efficiency	Low	Med	High
Liquidity	High	Low	Med
Ability to gear	Low	High	High
Fun	Low	Med	High
Hassle factor	Low	High	Med

Each investment class has its place. Shares might be difficult to understand and the returns are lumpy and uncertain, but to reject them as an investment is to reject the profits that businesses make. If you feel the fear of shares, the best way to overcome it is to think of them as owning a part of a business: you don't own 'shares' – you own a business (or at least a part of one).

RETURNS FROM SHARES

It is easy to give the historic returns from shares, and those encouraging people into the sharemarket often do so to show how good those returns have been. However, in many ways such figures are misleading. The returns that are given can easily be manipulated to show whatever is wanted. The start and/or finish date for when you were supposed to be investing can be arranged to show as great a return as desired. This is one of the reasons why I do not buy into the debate as to which is the better investment, shares or property. The statistics can be fixed to show pretty well whatever you like. In any event, past returns are just that – past. You are investing for the future.

Nevertheless, the returns from shares have been very good in the past and that is likely to continue. Businesses will continue to make profits to a greater or lesser extent and as an investor you should have a share of those profits. Whether shares will return 5% or 20% p.a. is of course unknown. However, it is likely that over a 10-year period the returns from shares will beat interest-earning deposits and property. And, of course, at any time shares can boom in value – a boom that you will want to be part of. The downturns that have occurred around the world do, of course, increase the opportunities for investors. History shows that markets perform very strongly when a country comes out of a recession, typically producing returns of 40% in the year that the recession ends.

The returns from shares come in two ways:

1. **Dividends.** This is the part of the company's profits that is paid out to shareholders. Most companies pay out 30–50% of their profits by way of dividends, although this varies greatly: Guinness Peat Group pays out very little in dividends while Michael Hill pays out 60% of its profits to shareholders. The balance of the company's profit is retained by the company and used for expansion.

   The receipt of dividends can in some cases make up a large

proportion of the total return to shareholders, and some people go into the market as much for those dividends as anything else. At the time of writing you could buy a basket of six to eight quite good companies and get an average dividend yield of close to 8%. That's not a bad return for an investor requiring a cash return at a time when you would only get 5% by putting your money in the bank. If you reinvest your dividends back into the company, you will get a compounding effect and your investment will grow rapidly.

There are sharemarket investors who go almost exclusively for high-dividend-yielding shares. Some of these are people who require cash income to live on. However, there are others who take their dividends and reinvest them. Generally companies which pay out most of their profit in dividends and sell on very high dividend yields have quite low growth rates. This is because the market sees little likely growth in profits or share price and pushes the price down to a level where the dividend yield is good enough to attract buyers. Some investors take advantage of this, enjoying the 10–12% (or more) that they get as a return by way of dividends and expect little growth – with 10–12% returns from their dividends they have a reasonable enough investment even without any growth. While this is by no means my own preferred strategy, for most people such a basket of shares would certainly beat money in the bank.

2. **Capital gains.** The rise in share price is what most people are looking for from their share investments. It is probably fair to say that most investors expect the bulk of their returns to come from rising share prices. Some of the growth in share price may come about simply because the company retains a proportion of the profit. Retained profit will increase the net assets of the company whether it is used to retire debt, buy more plant and equipment, increase stock levels, or whether that retained profit simply sits in the bank account.

However, most of the increase in share price will come about because the company is managing to increase its profitability. Whether the company pays out the higher profit as a greater dividend or keeps it to fund even more growth, you as a shareholder have a share in that extra profit. Because the business is making more money, new shareholders will pay more for the shares through the sharemarket. Again, you have a compounding effect here – part of the growth in profits will be retained by the company and those retained profits are used to make even more money.

Growth in profit leads to growth in share price – the two interact in this way in a formula explained in Way Three. Of course, a fall in profit will conversely lead to a fall in share price.

DIVIDEND GROWTH

If the company manages to increase its profit, it will also probably increase its dividend. This increasing dividend becomes a major part of your overall return, especially if that increased dividend is compared to the price you originally paid. It can make your return look very good indeed compared to other investments. Over the years, if a company increases its profits and dividend, the dividend yield can be very high based on the original purchase price of the shares.

SOMETHING FOR EVERYONE

One of the good things about the sharemarket is that it can be all things to all people. There is a spectrum for sharemarket operators, ranging from speculating day traders to the people who buy a diversified spread of shares and lock them away in a drawer for 20 years. Each group is at the extreme and opposite ends of the spectrum; each can profit from shares (although I would bet on the group holding quality shares for 20 years rather than the day traders!). In between are the rest of us, some tending more towards opportunistic trading, others more long-term investors. Many people are thrashing around in the middle, doing a bit of everything but often not doing it well.

A lot of investors are all over the place. They tend not to be planned in their approach and mix things up. There is little focus on what they are doing or why. In fact, many people in the sharemarket are simply chancers – people who are scouring the markets looking for a quick buck.

PLAN FOR PROFIT

I think it is important, in fact crucial, to plan how you are going to operate in the sharemarket: to work out what sort of person you are, to think about your age and stage of life, to decide what you enjoy doing and to set a strategy so that the sharemarket will give you what you need. That may be to grow your wealth, to supplement your income in retirement, or to make you rich. The sharemarket can give you any of these – but you need to decide which it is going to be *before* you start buying. A little bit of time spent planning will give you a single purpose, rather than a confused mix of a dozen purposes or, as is more common, no declared purpose at all.

The sharemarket can be all things to all people but not all at once. It is certainly possible to divide your capital and use some for trading and some for long-term investing. This is really having two portfolios, each with a separate purpose that you can concentrate on. In fact, splitting capital like this is sensible and something which many of us who want to beat the market do. However, in doing so it is important that the two portfolios are not mixed up – they need to be kept separate.

> **The sharemarket can be all things to all people but not all at once.**

This book is not for the day traders – those who buy and sell shares on a daily (or even hourly) basis, looking at the slightest price wrinkle that might make them a dollar. These people spend 12 hours a day peering at computer screens barely daring to leave their desks for a toilet break. It seems apparent that even when the markets boom and with an incredible amount of hard work put in by many day traders, few of them make much money. It is a fairly safe bet that, with the major slump in values, most of the day traders who were around a few years ago have now found proper jobs. In any case, this book would have been little help to day traders.

Nor is this book really for those who want to perform to the market average. That is easy to do and does not require a book. Instead it is for those who want to understand how things work, to outperform and profit beyond the average without giving up their day jobs to stare at computer screens.

CHAPTER TWO

From the beginning – companies and the market

The sharemarket exists as a way of buying and selling bits of businesses, and for those businesses to raise capital. You have to know what these 'bits of businesses' actually are and to understand the mechanism that is used to buy and sell them.

Mostly, businesses are owned through limited liability companies. It is true that some are owned through trusts (Kiwi Income Property is actually a trust rather than a company). However, the majority of securities that are listed on the NZX are shares in limited liability companies. A company is a way for a group of people to get together to jointly own a business. The shareholders have limited liability – they are not liable for the company's debts and can only lose the money that they have put in as share capital. People put their money in and own a share (or shares) of the business in proportion to what they have invested. This has always been the way – people have for centuries (even millennia) formed partnerships, joined in with others and so pooled their resources to own a business. It is a very reasonable thing to do – if someone wants to own a particular type of business but lacks the cash to buy it, it seems a good idea to bring others in to help them. Of course in bringing in others, you have to give up some ownership. The sharemarket is the place where you can raise capital and then, later on, buy or sell it. The sharemarket is a market for capital.

> **The sharemarket is a market for capital.**

STARTING UP A COMPANY

Say that a few people have an idea for a business. Ten of them get together, form a company and put in $10,000 – each of them has 10,000 shares at $1. The company is formed with an initial capital of $100,000 (10 x $10,000), it is given a name and the documents are signed. These documents include the company's constitution. This is just like the constitution of, say, a golf club, and sets out the rules for the company (how many directors it might have, what sort of businesses it will own, voting rights of shareholders and so on). The company is registered with the Companies Office and any member of the public can see who the shareholders are, who the directors are, read the constitution, etc. Once the company is registered, its ownership and constitutional activities are available for public scrutiny (although commercially sensitive issues are not).

DIRECTORS

The 10 shareholders of the company realise that it is not practicable for them all to have a say in the running of the company – they cannot get everyone together each time a decision has to be made. So, a board of directors is elected by the shareholders. This could be three or four of the shareholders who will then run the company. The 10 shareholders might also choose to appoint an outsider, someone who is not a shareholder but who has a lot of business experience. Directors do not need to be shareholders and indeed often are not. The directors may also, on behalf of the company, appoint managers and other employees who will get on with running the company.

The shareholders are still the ultimate controllers of the company – it is their company. They will get together for an annual meeting (to elect directors and to review the company's performance) and might also hold a meeting if big asset acquisitions or disposals were contemplated, extra finance had to be arranged or some other major transaction proposed. The shareholders elect and ultimately control the directors, although at times when the shareholders are not in a properly called general meeting, the directors run the company. Again, this is no different from the golf club – a committee is elected to make ongoing decisions on behalf of the club and its members, bearing in mind the likely wishes of the members.

COMPANY FINANCES

The company has $100,000 of share capital to fund its operations. It may increase this by borrowing from a bank or finance company and use both its borrowings and its original share capital to buy assets and to provide working capital for a business that it owns. It may be that this capital is sufficient. However, in most cases businesses require more capital over time for replacing assets, going into new areas of commerce or to fund growth. There are three ways that a company can obtain more capital:

1. **Borrow more money.** There are obvious limitations to this as banks and others will not lend to a point where they regard borrowings as too high. Quite probably, this company with $100,000 of share capital could not borrow much more than $150,000. That would mean that it could not have a total of more than $250,000 of capital (its $100,000 of share capital plus $150,000 of borrowings).
2. **Retain its profits.** The 10 shareholders have put their money into the company so that they will receive the profits by way of dividends. However, nearly all companies retain part of their profits and add it to their capital. By retaining some of their profits they increase the capital of the company. If the company made $50,000 profit after tax, it might elect to pay half of that profit ($25,000) to the shareholders as dividends (each would receive $2500) and retain the other half. Its capital would now be:

Share capital	$100,000
Borrowings	$150,000
Retained profits	$ 25,000
	$275,000

3. **Sell more shares.** The company might issue more shares to other investors. It could increase its share capital from $100,000 to $200,000. However, before it can do this, the existing shareholders would need to agree that it was a good idea and then the company has to find other investors who are prepared to put their money in. This is where the sharemarket (the market for capital) comes in – the sharemarket as an institution exists so that companies can raise more capital (as well as allowing existing shareholders to sell out if they want to). The company might decide to raise more capital through an Initial Public Offering (IPO) and have its shares listed on the sharemarket.

SELLING SHARES TO THE PUBLIC

There are two ways that shares might be sold to the public:

1. The company itself may issue new shares. In effect, the company sells these shares and it gets the proceeds from the sale. The money from the sale of its shares is added to its capital. When you buy new shares like this, your money is going into the company that you now own a part of and that money will go to buy more assets, fund growth, etc.

2. Some of the existing shareholders might sell all or part of their shares. This means that those shareholders receive the proceeds from the sale, but the company itself is unaffected. This was how Contact Energy was sold to the public and floated on the sharemarket. The Government was the shareholder. Through its brokers, the Government organised the sale of the company's shares to the public (in a blaze of publicity) and banked the proceeds.

Sometimes companies are listed on the sharemarket in a combination of the company issuing new shares (and receiving the proceeds from that) at the same time as one or more of the shareholders sell out. Sky Television's float was organised like this – new shares were issued by the company, the proceeds going back to the company, and at the same time Television New Zealand sold its stake.

INITIAL PUBLIC OFFERINGS (IPOs)

Most new companies come onto the market with an issue of new shares. The company appoints a broker and registers a prospectus and then goes out to promote the company to sell the shares in it. Note that the sharebrokers now have a selling job to do – and like anyone in sales they are going to accentuate the positive and eliminate (or bury) the negative. Buying shares in an IPO is like buying anything: as the buyer you need to beware!

So that the sale of shares is fair and the public can make an informed decision on whether or not to buy shares in a new issue, the company must register a prospectus with the Securities Commission and issue an investment statement. These documents contain some of the fundamental information that anyone would want before investing: the company's finances, what the capital that is raised will be used for, who the directors are, past performance of the company, business prospects, risks involved, etc. The investment statement is usually a shorter version of the prospectus, containing less information, and is often like a glossy magazine – it is really the company's sales pitch for the sale of its shares. It is the investment statement that most members of the public see, although anyone can ask for a copy of the prospectus if they want.

The brokers going out to sell the company's shares will approach a number of people and organisations:

1. **Institutions.** Large insurance companies, banks and fund managers buy for the funds that they manage and are often the first target of the organising brokers. If they can persuade the institutions to buy, they will be able to place large numbers of shares with them.

2. **Other brokers.** Although it is not as common as it once was, the

organising broker will sometimes sell an allocation of shares to other brokers to sell on to their clients.

3. **The public.** The organising broker will mount a campaign through the media (advertising, press releases, seminars) to encourage the public to subscribe for shares.

UNDERWRITING

Sometimes the organising broker will agree with the company to underwrite the issue of new shares (for a fee). This means that the organising broker is effectively guaranteeing to sell all of the shares that are going to be issued. If the underwriting broker cannot sell all of the shares, the broker ends up owning the unsold ones. This is a very bad sign for the issue. If the share issue closes undersubscribed, it means that there has not been sufficient demand for the shares because institutions and the public do not think much of the company and its prospects. This leaves the organising broker with a lot of shares it does not really want. It will try to sell them at a reasonable price when the company lists on the sharemarket. These unsold shares will overhang the market for days, weeks or even months, depressing the share price until the supply is exhausted.

LISTING

Once the shares are sold and the issue has closed, the company will apply to have its shares listed on the sharemarket. Most prospectuses foreshadow this by saying that following the issue, there will be an application to the NZX to have the shares listed. Of course, there can be no guarantee that the shares will be listed although they almost always are. Whether or not a company's shares can be listed is not up to the company – it is up to the NZX.

The NZX does not have to provide a market for a company's shares. The NZX has rules and regulations and the issue of shares must meet certain criteria. These rules are in the first instance mostly about making sure that the shares are spread amongst a wide number of different people so that there is a good and efficient market, and about providing the market with regular and accurate information on how the company is performing.

Following a successful issue (i.e. after the new issued shares are sold to a good spread of investors) it is almost a foregone conclusion that the NZX will accept quotes (both buy and sell quotes) for the issue. This means that any member of the public, through a broker, can put in a 'bid' (a price at which they want to buy) or an 'offer' (a price at which they want to sell). This, in a technical sense, is of no concern to the company. It has raised its capital, banked the cash and its job is now to get on with its business. The quotes on the sharemarket are the concern of the shareholders – it is the shareholders who are buying and selling (and only incidentally the shares of the company concerned). Of course the directors and managers of the company will usually have more than a passing interest in what is happening on the market. In fact they may often run the company with an eye to boosting the share price. Nevertheless, strictly speaking the company itself is not affected in its trading by the share price (although a high share price does make it easy for the company to make another issue of its shares to raise more capital).

STAGGING

Stagging (or being a stag) is to buy shares prior to a listing through an IPO with the intention of selling them immediately on listing. Often that means selling on the day of listing, certainly within a few days. Stagging is a very profitable sideline for anyone interested in the sharemarket. If you bought every new company that was coming onto the market and sold on the day of listing you would certainly make money. Sure, you would lose out on the odd one that comes on at a discount to the listing price, but overall you would be ahead (the most recent IPO, Kathmandu, saw profits for stags).

> **Stagging is a very profitable sideline for anyone interested in the sharemarket.**

The key to the success of new listings is the success (or otherwise) of the organising brokers in being able to promote the prospects of the company so that there is more demand for shares than they can supply. When this happens the issue is said to close oversubscribed. Sometimes issues close several times oversubscribed – the organising brokers have 100 million shares to sell but receive applications for, say, 200 million shares. Such happenings are of great joy to the stags who have managed to get some shares – the company is bound to list at a premium. Of course, if the brokers cannot create enough demand and fail to sell all of the shares on offer, there will not be anything for the stags (except a loss).

There are two problems with making good profits from stagging:

1. If a new issue is really popular, it is hard to get any sort of meaningful quantity of shares. Sometimes you may get none at all; sometimes the issuer will scale back applications and give people only a fraction of what they want. With Contact Energy's float, applications were scaled back to around 300 shares each. This prompted people to make applications in as many different names as possible: their children, company, family trust, spouse, parents – an application form was filled out in each name so that the family would get as many shares as possible. This works quite well when there is a public pool – shares which are allocated to be sold directly to the public. It may be a bit messy, but the profits are often worthwhile.

   However, many shares in IPOs are sold via brokers. The organising broker will sell shares to its clients and may make a firm allocation to other brokers. If the issue is popular and therefore likely to be profitable, there is a mad scramble to do what you can to get shares. Any broker who gets a firm allocation will deal these shares out selectively – the best clients will get them. Some people use several different brokers and so hope to get more shares in new listings by getting a few from each one. That will work for some new issues but probably will not for the really popular ones. Shares in the best new listings are like gold – they will be dealt out to people who have done good consistent business with the broker. I think that you are better to use just one or two brokers predominantly, becoming a good and valued client.

2. The second problem with buying new listings is that with some no firm price is given before you have to commit yourself to buy. This is 'open pricing' – and I hate it. Retail investors send in an application with their money. At the same time the issuer (through its brokers) takes bids from institutional investors. This 'book building' process with the institutions tells the company what the demand for its shares is and the price is finally set by it. The first way that retail investors hear about what price they are being forced to pay is in the news media. By that time they are committed – effectively the company banks their cheque and decides how many shares it will send. Contact Energy was floated like this. A price guide of 240–300c was given but demand was so great (good advertising and PR) that the final price was struck at 315c. Personally, I like to know the price of something before I buy it – I have never much liked this open-pricing method of listing shares.

> I don't think that I would have bought Contact Energy at 315c.

MAKE UP YOUR MIND

When buying into an IPO, decide at the beginning what you are going to do with the shares. Do not think that you can wait until the shares have listed and then decide. If you have bought to stag, sell them straight away. If the shares list at a discount, so be it – take your loss rather than waiting to see if they will rise. If they list at a premium, take your profit (and pay your tax – see Chapter Four). Dithering and waiting to see what happens does not work.

There are two other ways that companies may sell shares and raise capital:

1. Private placement

The company, usually through brokers or investment bankers, might approach institutions with a view to placing some shares with them. This is an issue of shares only offered to that institution and not to other shareholders, nor to the public. Such placements are often at a discount to the market (around 5%), which is of course attractive to the institution.

This is beneficial to the company because it is a quick and easy way to raise capital. It will pay a fee to the brokers but there are no advertising or prospectus costs. Private placements are usually only possible when the company is doing well and its share price is strong. This is not a means of last-resort financing. Although the institution may have a 5% discount to act as a buffer, it will still want to have a very good look at what it is buying.

2. Cash issues

This is when a company offers new shares to its shareholders in proportion to their existing shareholdings. That means that the company might offer one new share for five already held at a certain price. This price will be at a discount to the price on the market.

You are under no obligation to buy any new shares. However, if you don't, your shareholding will be diluted because other shareholders may buy and more shares will be issued. Most cash issues are 'renounceable' offers – that is, you can renounce the right to buy more shares and sell that 'right' on the market. After a cash issue is announced, there is a period of a few weeks when the rights can be traded on the sharemarket. If you do not want to put more money into the company, you should arrange to sell your rights. Some other investor will buy your rights to new shares, pay the company the amount required and be issued these new shares.

However, that will mean that you have less money in the company. This is because after the cash issue there are more shares on issue and the share price will fall accordingly. Up until the entitlement date, the shares will be quoted 'cum issue' (CI) which means that they are with the issue, i.e. they carry the right to buy new shares. After the entitlement date they go ex-issue (XI) and the price will fall to reflect the dilution. You need to work out the theoretical ex-issue price.

> ***EXAMPLE***
>
> A shareholder has 1000 shares when the company announces a cash issue of one for five at 200c. The prevailing market price is 600c.
>
> 1000 'old' shares at 600c = $ 6000
>
> 200 'new' shares at 200c = $ 400
>
> Shareholder now has 1200 with a total value of $6400.
>
> Average value is $6400 ÷ 1,200 = 533.
>
> Theoretical ex price is 533c.

Some people who want to keep their total amount of investment in the company the same will sell some of their rights and use the proceeds of that sale to take up the remainder of the shares that are offered them. The price for the rights on the market is usually approximately the price of the head shares on the market less the exercise price (the price that the company is selling its shares at).

For example, a company makes a cash issue, selling shares at 200c. Its market price is 460c. The price of the rights will, therefore, be around 260c.

TIME TO BUY

The rights trading period can represent an excellent time to buy into a company (and conversely a very poor time to sell). Many shareholders are not able to exercise all their rights and have to sell some. Therefore, large amounts of a company's capital come onto the market for sale. This relatively high number of shares and rights to be sold has a depressing effect on the company's share price. This is particularly so if the cash issue is a big one raising a lot of cash, or if the company has made regular cash issues in the past. Companies which approach their shareholders frequently, calling for large amounts of cash through issues, sometimes find their shareholders becoming increasingly reluctant to take them up. However, cash issues do constitute a good way for a company to bring in extra capital. Providing the company is using the cash that is raised wisely, the growth of the company will continue and the shareholders who have taken up their rights will in time be rewarded.

> **The rights trading period can represent an excellent time to buy into a company.**

BONUS ISSUES

While this is not really a means of capital raising, bonus issues do happen quite frequently and need to be mentioned here. A bonus issue occurs when the company issues shares to its existing shareholders free.

The new shares are issued in proportion to the shareholder's holding at a given date. So a one-for-four bonus issue means that for each four shares a shareholder has, the company will give one share free. If the shareholder has 200 shares, he or she will be given 50 shares free.

As soon as the bonus issue is announced, the shares are traded on the exchange, CB, that is, 'cum bonus' (or with bonus). The shares are traded with their bonus until the entitlement date. At that date, everyone with shares in the company participates in the bonus issue.

After the entitlement date the shares are traded XB. This stands for 'ex bonus' (or without bonus). The shares that are ex bonus will be cheaper than those which were cum bonus because when the bonus issue is made, there are more of the company's shares on issue. This dilutes the earnings per share, there being more shares taking a part of the company's profit. This reduces the share price and there is a downward adjustment to reflect the fact that there are more shares on issue. This new, lower share price after the entitlement date is the 'theoretical ex price'. The theoretical ex price is the price which would be required to keep the shareholder's holding at the same value.

EXAMPLE

A shareholder has 1000 shares when a bonus issue of 1 for 4 is announced. On the entitlement date the market price is 600c.

1000 'old' shares at 600c	=	$ 6000
250 'new' shares free		nil
1250 shares with total value	=	$ 6000

Average value of each share is $4.80 (6000 ÷ 1250).

Theoretical ex price is 480c.

Instead of having a holding of 1000 shares at 600c each, the shareholder has 1250 shares at 480c each. The result, assuming that the value of the holding remains the same, is more shares at a cheaper price.

This lower price can be of benefit to both the company and its shareholders. The lower price attracts more people to buy shares in the company, thus pushing the price back up. Many people will not (or in some cases cannot) buy high-priced shares. They believe that shares of a high dollar value are 'too expensive'. This is not very sensible as often the higher-priced shares represent much better value in terms of earnings and assets. These fundamentals – assets and earnings ratios – are the most important things in buying shares. It is, however, human nature to believe that you are better to buy company A whose share price is 50c rather than company B whose share price is 500c. An individual with $2000 to invest often buys company A because he or she can buy 4,000 shares instead of buying 400 shares in company B. There is nothing logical about this – but human nature does not always put logic first.

Companies realise that people do not buy shares of high dollar value so easily and thus have bonus issues regularly to keep the price from getting too high. It should also be noted that without bonus issues (or cash issues, or the splitting of par value) long-established companies that have grown over the years would have astronomical share prices. For example, Warren Buffett's company, Berkshire Hathaway, has a share price of US$110,000. This is a ludicrous situation prohibiting most people from becoming shareholders. (You can buy Berkshire Hathaway 'B' shares which are at a very modest US$370 each.)

The market usually reacts well to the announcement of a bonus issue. Bonus issues formalise a company's good fortunes – it is usually only companies that are doing well that make bonus issues. People buy the company's shares in the expectation that the shares will rise soon after they go ex bonus. Guinness Peat Group announces a 1:10 bonus issue most years, and the shareholders look forward to the extra value of their holdings as the number of shares that they have goes up, but the share price does not usually long stay 10% under the CB price as it should.

> The market usually reacts well to the announcement of a bonus issue.

REDUCTION OF CAPITAL

A company can decide to reduce its capital by buying its shares from its shareholders. The company may return capital to shareholders directly in proportion to their shareholding or it may go onto the sharemarket and buy its own shares.

This is generally a very positive sign for a company. Buying back its own shares is sending a signal that the company is doing very well and is well cashed up. It is also saying that in buying back its own shares the company has nothing better to do with its capital – its own shares are the best investment it can find. This of course tends to support the company's share price at a high level – something that is very good for shareholders!

In the final analysis, the success of all capital raisings will depend on the strength and performance of the business(es) that the company owns. The issuing company and its brokers and investment bankers might get away with selling shares in a dud with hype and marketing once or twice. However, they will not do so for long.

You as a potential buyer need to realise that you are being sold something and therefore approach the possible purchase with suitable cynicism. Brokers and investment bankers are good at selling and marketing (that's how they make a living). The brokers may not be on your side – they are likely to earn far more in fees from organising issues than they are ever going to earn from you.

Having suggested some cynicism, I do believe that you should look to take up most if not all IPOs that become available. You will probably want to avoid new listings in property (they seldom come onto the market at a premium). However, any business that is being listed on the main board deserves your scrutiny and probably your investment.

You should look to take up most if not all IPOs that become available.

CHAPTER THREE

Brokers, processes and management

Brokers are a key part of this whole process. Not only are they at the centre of things as companies try to raise capital by issuing shares to the public, but they are also involved in making the market for shares, arranging for buyers to meet sellers and organising the transactions.

Brokers control the market. They are the people best informed on what is going on and very influential in investors' buy-and-sell decisions. Brokers visit companies, know the managers and directors, talk to institutional and retail investors and meet with each other. Although legally brokers are acting as agents, taking clients' orders and transacting business on their behalf, the reality is that their influence is so pervasive that very little happens without them.

Most of the big brokerage houses have investment banking divisions, so that along with their standard broking work (buying and selling shares for you) they are also dealing with companies to arrange new issues of shares, private placements, cash issues, etc. In effect, the brokerage house is working with the company, saying that it will be able to arrange to place (i.e. sell) shares to its own clients.

Brokers also put out reports on the company and give 'buy' and 'sell' recommendations to you, the client (and take a fee from you if you go ahead with a trade). There are supposed to be 'Chinese walls' between the investment banking division and the broking division but these are often flimsy. You very rarely see brokers recommending that their clients sell a particular stock and it is even rarer to hear them roundly criticise companies. Brokerage houses cannot afford to insult companies by putting a sell recommendation on them (let alone say that a company is a dog) when no doubt they will want to do business with them in the future, to organise a new issue or a merger or acquisition.

BROKER RECOMMENDATIONS

Brokers try to get around this by speaking in code.

Brokers' recommendations are often couched in these terms:

Strong buy
Buy
Accumulate
Overweight
Hold
Underweight
Sell

Of all of them, the 'sell' recommendation is used least. In fact, studies in New Zealand and around the world show that less than 2% of brokers' recommendations are to sell. This may be for three reasons:

1. The brokerage house does not want to insult companies that it might get investment banking business from.

2. Brokers tend to sell the idea of buying because it has a positive and optimistic flavour and it is easier and more profitable to do so.

3. People should do more buying than selling. Provided they have bought the right shares, they will seldom want to sell them.

I think all of these different recommendations (buy, hold, overweight, etc) are ridiculous for small private investors. There should simply be a buy or a sell recommendation – you are either a bull or a bear. To buy or to hold shares is to be a bull; to sell and not hold is to be a bear. People need to (and do) make up their own minds. To recommend 'hold' is at best indecisiveness, at worst the brokers' euphemism (or code) for something else.

Brokers use terms like 'hold' or 'underweight' not because they can't make up their minds. They know that you can't be both a bull and a bear. They do so because they have to speak to their clients in code to avoid upsetting their other clients who are the companies involved.

> Brokers' recommendations are only the starting point for your own investigation and analysis.

This is why brokers' recommendations are only the starting point for your own investigation and analysis. You need to see other views, whether they are from other brokers, tip sheets or the business media. This is especially so if the broker that you are using is involved in investment banking or if the broker is new to you and you have not yet built up a level of trust.

There has been a growing trend within brokerage houses at a retail level to try to get funds under management rather than fees from simple transaction brokerage. This represents a change in business model for most of the bigger broking firms as they become more like financial planners and investment advisors than sharebrokers. In fact, some of the large sharebrokers now employ financial planners who offer comprehensive financial advisory services.

These sharebroking houses now offer to look after your investment portfolio for you, buying and selling investments on your behalf and acting as custodians of your investments. All of this means that there is something of a convergence going on between sharebrokers and other investment advisers. However, there is an important difference: only brokers who are members of the NZX can transact share sales and purchases for you, and in spite of many of them adopting a new business model, they will continue to offer this service – for a fee, of course.

FEES

Right from the start, let me say that I am happy to pay a good broker a good fee. Brokers only get paid when something is bought or sold – they get a commission, usually a percentage of the transaction, ranging from 1.5% (for small orders), down to 0.7% or less (for big ones). Some brokers charge a flat transaction fee (say, $30) regardless of size. Brokers do not charge for their time or for advice – they only get paid if something happens.

> I am happy to pay a good broker a good fee.

That's fine with me and I happily pay for the service. However, it does, in appearance at least, mean that the broker is not an independent adviser whose only interest is the client's wellbeing. The broker, in taking a commission, is a party to the transaction and has an interest in the transaction itself. This is not an interest in the quality of the transaction, but in the fact that a transaction does take place – because if it doesn't, the broker earns nothing. In this respect, they are no different from real estate agents. Although with all of the brokers I have dealt with, I have always felt that they were on my side, people have to be suspicious, especially on first starting to use a new broker.

WHAT SORT OF BROKER?

Your most fundamental decision when choosing a broker is whether to go with one who gives research advice or one who does not. Full-service brokers of course cost more. They have had their market share eroded a little by their no-frills, no-advice, orders-only colleagues and by brokers taking orders via the Internet. The trend away from full-service broking is quite possibly alarming to those who offer that service. However, I do not think they will die out.

People using no-advice brokers must be very confident of their own ability to pick shares by themselves. They must be people who consider themselves skilled enough to keep their own counsel and who put no or little value on what others might think. In doing so, they save money (a good thing to do!). However, they may also be missing opportunities.

Even though I regard myself as a reasonably skilled share investor, I still use a full-service broker.

What I get from a full-service broker is:

- Another opinion – I may have decided what I want to buy but it's always good to get another view. I value that other view and am prepared to pay for it.
- The depth of the market at the time of buying. I can see the best buy quote and the best sell quote by going on-line (I use ***www.sharechat.co.nz*** or ***www.findata.co.nz***). However, I can't find out whether there are lots of sellers above that level or lots of buyers below it (see *Meet the Market* on pages 42–44).
- Research – this is on an ongoing regular basis as the broker does it, or I can ask for anything that they have on my target company.
- Tips on other things that I should look at whenever I am buying. I always ask what else I should be looking at. This sometimes yields good profits.

I think that these things are worth paying for. While I might sometimes use a no-frills broker to sell if that is what I am determined to do, I really like the idea of having someone to talk to about what I am thinking of doing. Share investing is often a fairly solitary activity – paying for another opinion from a good and trusted broker suits me very well.

CHOOSING A BROKER

I like a broker who I can chat with, who will give me personal service. That's why I prefer full-service brokers. I try to make my business worthwhile to the broker (so that I get better service) and generally do not have more than one broker. While there is nothing to stop you having as many different brokers as you like, it has always seemed sensible to me to consolidate all your business with just one (or maybe two). Having several may place you on a lot of mailing lists and therefore give you access to more research and information, though such information is now not difficult to come by. Regular contact with one good broker and a good working relationship is to me more important.

> I like a broker who will give me personal service.

Perhaps the main thing in choosing a broker is trust. Finding someone who you can trust is ultimately a matter of judgement. The first step will probably come from a referral or personal recommendation from a friend, relative or colleague. The second step is to go into the broker's office and meet with him or her. Most people transact most of their business over the phone (I do), but an initial meeting is important to develop a relationship.

I think that the individual broker is more important than the firm that the broker is with. While some firms will have better research than others, better contacts and perhaps better access to new listings, I think that a good personal relationship based on trust is more important. In the past, I have followed individual brokers when they have left one firm and gone to another. I know that this desire for a personal relationship goes against the trend towards Internet no-advice broking with all of the cost savings – perhaps I'm a bit old-fashioned! However, for me the comfort of dealing with a real person who is prepared to spend a bit of time gossiping makes up for that cost saving. One good piece of advice: just one good deal can yield profits that make the cost savings from no-advice broking look like small beer.

> The individual broker is more important than the firm that the broker is with.

THE MARKET

Brokers make the market. Through the NZX they are responsible for making sure that anyone who wants to buy can get in touch with anyone who wants to sell. Brokers act as agents for their clients, taking their orders and 'advertising' the shares for sale or the desire to buy. They do this on a network of computers, arranging the 'meeting' of the buy and the sell parties and the contract for sale and purchase. All you have to do is give your broker the order. There are two main types of order you can give your broker:

- At market. This means that the broker will do his best to buy or sell at the best price and the shares will be bought or sold as close to the price that prevailed at the time of the order. There is of course some uncertainty, especially if the shares start to move one way or the other quickly.
- Limit order. This gives the broker an order to buy or sell at a particular price (or better if he can). While this takes out the uncertainty, there is a risk that the market moves and you never get your order actioned. For example, say you give an order to your broker to sell 1000 Telecom at 480c. If there are no buyers at that level and the share price drops to 460c, you are left stranded still with your Telecom shares.

MEET THE MARKET

I always like to meet the market. If I wanted to sell Fletcher Building shares I would phone my broker and ask him what he has Fletcher Building at. He would look at his screen and tell me the depth of the market. It might look like this:

	BIDS			**ASKS**	
BNAME	VOLUME	PRICE	PRICE	VOLUME	BNAME
FNZW	8039	790	791	10000	
	1250	790	792	5000	
	343	789	793	10000	

BIDS			ASKS		
BNAME	VOLUME	PRICE	PRICE	VOLUME	BNAME
	8615	788	795	4000	
	2500	785	796	5000	
	600	782	799	2100	
	10630	780	800	8232	
	500	780	803	94	
	795	776	804	2700	
	6450	775	804	250	
	1500	775	805	2500	
	500	775	805	19700	FNZW
	1308	760	805	400	
	1000	760	808	1000	
FNZW	1000	760	809	816	
FNZW	2200	750	809	1000	
	1333	750	809	20000	FNZW
FNZW	3300	750	809	1302	
	650	748	810	1485	
	1500	747	810	1485	

This gives me a snapshot of the market for Fletcher Building shares at that moment. In fact this is the market at that time, a statement of all of those wanting to buy or sell with the number of shares wanting to be bought or that are for sale. At a glance, I can see that there are the same number of sellers (asks) and buyers (bids), and although that could change at any moment (more buyers or sellers could come in), it indicates that Fletcher Building's share price is reasonably balanced. This look at the depth of the market gives me some choices as to how I can go about selling:

1. I could put a sell order in at, say, 795c and wait and hope. To be successful I would have to wait until 19,000 shares had been sold at that price because I would be last in line (shares at the same price are sold in the order that they came in). I could get greedier and say sell at 800c. At that price there are a lot of sellers in front of me and the buyers look a long way below – I

might have to wait days or weeks and of course might never manage the sale.

2. I could ask to sell at 791c and wait. Now I am hoping that one of the buyers at 790c will move up and take my shares at 791c. There is a fairly good chance that one of them will do that although I will have to wait for a bit. The risk is of course that none of the buyers moves but a seller comes in to sell 10,000 shares at 790c. Straightaway that seller would sell 8,039 of his shares and would have the remaining 1,961 now sitting for sale at 790c. I am now stranded on 791c and again might be in for a long wait.

3. I could say sell at 790c. That would mean that my shares would be sold immediately at that price (because there is a buyer at 790c). Certainly by wanting the deal done now I don't get as much money – but I know that the shares are gone and am not exposed to the risk of the market moving significantly against me.

I usually take option 3 – I meet the market and get the deal done. I don't care much about a few cents either way – regardless of whether I am buying or selling, certainty is more important to me. If I am buying something, whether I get shares at 146c or 148c should not make much difference in the long run. It is more important that I own the shares. In the above example, selling 1,000 Fletcher Building shares, the difference in what I would receive between selling at 790c or 791c is $100. That is not really very important.

I always try to have the sale or purchase made before I come off the phone. I may not get the best deal but I like the peace of mind. Meeting the market and getting the deal done gives certainty, allows you to move on to other business and means that you can take other opportunities.

CONTRACTS

When your broker has bought or sold shares for you, you will receive a contract note which confirms the agreement for sale or purchase of shares. The contract note tells you:

- What shares you have bought or sold.
- The quantity of shares.
- The price paid or received.
- The date they were bought or sold.
- The amount of brokerage.
- Settlement date (if you have purchased shares).

The settlement date is the date by which you must get a cheque to the brokers or pay by on-line banking. Generally you have to do that within three days. Sometimes this may not work very well (you may be travelling, for example), so many people set up an account with their broker in which funds are kept. This is convenient as the broker can simply draw on funds. If you are selling one lot of shares and buying another lot your broker will usually allow you to offset the proceeds of the sale against the amount required. This means that you can effectively swap shares. If the shares that you are buying are offshore, the broker will usually arrange the foreign currency for you so that you only need to get New Zealand dollars to the broker to settle the purchase.

If you are selling shares, you should receive a cheque or electronic payment within a few days. If you have an account with your brokers, they will simply deposit funds into it. Regardless of whether you are buying or selling, when you receive a contract note, check it thoroughly. If there is anything incorrect on it, contact your broker immediately.

SHARE REGISTRY

Once you have bought the shares and paid for them, you will be registered as the owner. There are specialist share registry companies that provide this service for listed companies. They are charged with keeping a list (or a register) of all the shareholders of the company. This list of course changes all the time. Each share sale and purchase means that there is a change to the share register – someone new may come in as a shareholder (the buyer), someone may cease to be a shareholder (the seller), or there may simply be reductions or additions to the number of shares that various people own. All of this has to be accounted for, specifically the names of the shareholders and how many shares that they own. Companies like Computershare Registry Services and Link provide this share registration service.

Fortunately, these days companies do not issue share certificates to shareholders. Instead, in these days of 'scripless' trading you will receive notification of your shareholding from the share registry company that your newly purchased company uses. This notification will include an account showing the number of shares that you now own, your holder number and your FIN.

FIN is an acronym for Faster Identification Number. FASTER (Fully Automated Screen Trading and Electronic Registration) was the share registration system adopted by the NZX in place of share certificates to give us scripless trading. FASTER is a good name – the previous system of share certificates was extremely slow, inefficient and prone to mistakes. In fact just about any system would have been both faster and better.

You need an identification number to operate in the FASTER system because you have to give proof that you own the shares that you are selling. Previously, the share certificates that you held were proof of ownership – without such certificates you need an identification number which works the same as the PIN that you use to operate a bank card.

You cannot sell your shares without your holder number and your FIN – they prove who you are and no sharebroker will sell on your behalf without them. Keep your FIN and holder numbers safe, and keep them with you. You never know when you might want to sell and there is nothing more frustrating than wanting to sell but not having the numbers to hand.

The whole system for buying and selling shares (including FASTER) now works very efficiently. The system allows you to buy or sell almost instantly and there are few of the problems that used to occur with registration. Once you know how the system works and have used it a couple of times, it is simple and easy to administer your portfolio and takes little away from the real aim of share investors: identifying good companies.

CHAPTER FOUR

Tax – not a penny more nor a penny less

You can't invest in anything without thinking about tax. It makes no sense to win the investment game, only to lose to the IRD. Failure to arrange your affairs correctly can cost you a third or more of your profits in tax, or can result in a messy and expensive audit, maybe with penalties. Tax is something that you need to get right. You need to pay the right amount of tax – not a penny more nor a penny less.

It is hard to beat the market if you are giving a sizeable chunk to the Government. As a New Zealand investor you are fortunate in that with a bit of organisation you will not be heavily taxed on your share investments. New Zealand has no tax on capital gains and the days of double taxation of dividends are (fortunately) gone. Nevertheless, some people do pay more tax than they should. Sometimes this is because they have not structured their affairs correctly to minimise what they need to pay, while at other times it is because they have not paid enough tax and so are caught with tax penalties when audited.

> It is hard to beat the market if you are giving a sizeable chunk to the Government.

COMPARING TAX ON PROPERTY AND SHARES

Much is made of the tax efficiency of property as an investment. It is quite true that property is tax efficient, but shares are little if any less efficient. In fact, on just about all tax counts, shares are as good as property.

There are four main areas where property is tax efficient. Let's look at each of them and compare how shares are treated:

1. No capital gains tax. When you sell investment property, the profits are not taxable. This is certainly true for most property sales (excluding developers and traders) but it is just as true for share investments (see below).

2. You can claim the interest costs for borrowings on purchasing property. This is a major incentive for property investors and many borrow so much that they make a loss on their property – i.e. interest costs are greater than rental income, resulting in a tax refund. This is called negative gearing.

   However, the interest costs when borrowing to buy shares are also deductible and as outlined in Way Seven it is quite easy to do. Although people do not tend to borrow on shares as much as they do on property, I think it is just as valid to gear up long-term share investments as property investments, perhaps more so.

   Borrowing to buy shares or property has the effect of reducing the taxable income from dividends or rent but increases the amount of capital gains because you are purchasing more of the investments. In effect you are converting taxable income to non-taxable capital profit (provided you purchase the right thing!). This works just as well for shares as it does for property.

3. Property investors can depreciate for tax purposes their buildings and the chattels that are in them. This means that property investors may be cashflow positive (rent is greater than interest) but may still be in a tax loss position and still get a tax refund.

   You cannot depreciate your shareholdings. However, the companies that you own have already depreciated their assets. For example, a company may have a surplus of $100 million (before tax) but it offsets $20 million of depreciation and therefore only pays tax on $80 million. As a shareholder you have already had the tax benefit of depreciation – your company has already claimed it. This depreciation that is claimed by the company may not be as great as a property investor can claim but neither will be the depreciation recovered when the property is sold – property investors must pay tax on the amount of depreciation that they have claimed over the years. In other words, very often the claiming of depreciation is a tax deferral rather than a permanent saving.

4. When people buy investment property, they go into business. Because they are in business they can claim expenses that help them obtain their income. The obvious things like interest, rates, insurance and repairs are deductible. So too are less obvious expenses: items that had previously been personal non-deductible expenses may become tax-deductible ones. Things like the newspaper (to follow the property market), a part of motor vehicle expenses (to view properties), phone charges (to talk to tenants or real estate agents), home/office costs (an area at home used to run the rental property business) may all become tax deductible, at least in part.

However, property investors do not have this all to themselves – some share investors can also claim the costs that are needed to get their income (in this case their dividends or trading profits). Things like sharemarket newsletters, this book, part of their telephone costs, Internet connection, newspapers, business journals may be deductible. Smaller share investors could not make a case for claiming these items – 400 AMP shares that come from demutualisation would not put you into being in the business of share investing. However, those with big portfolios who are regularly trading can claim these things.

Shares are not really far behind property in terms of a favourable tax treatment. This is not to denigrate property as an investment – it certainly has its place. However, from a tax point of view, even though property investors may be a little better off, shares are still very tax efficient.

Let's look at how sharemarket profits are taxed and what you can do to minimise what you pay. Share profits come in two forms: profits from dividends and capital profits from selling what you have bought. Each is taxed in its own way.

CAPITAL PROFITS

When you sell your shares you will, if you have been skilful, make a profit. That profit may be taxable or it may not be. Whether it is or not depends on your *intention* and *purpose* at the time of purchase. Everything hinges on what you were thinking at that time.

Imagine that someone buys a truck and sells it later at a profit. Is that profit taxable? It may be or it may not:

1. If the person was a manufacturer of toothpicks and used the truck to deliver his goods to shops which stock toothpicks, the truck is a capital item used to obtain income. In this case the truck was not bought with the purpose to sell at a profit and therefore the profit is not taxable.

2. If the person was a truck dealer, the truck would have been part of his stock. He intends to buy and then sell trucks at a profit – that's how he makes a living. The sale of the truck would therefore be part of his income and therefore taxable.

Shares are no different. If you buy shares as capital items which are used to obtain income (through dividends), the profits from the sale of them are an unexpected (although welcome!) by-product and are not therefore taxable. However, if you deal in shares, buy with the intention of selling, they are like stock and you are therefore treated like any retailer or truck dealer.

The difference between trading and investment really comes down to your purpose and intention at the time that you bought the shares. If you buy the shares intending to hold them long term for their dividends and growth in dividends and any profit on sale was unplanned, then the profit is not taxable. On the other hand, if you purchased the shares intending to sell them on at a profit, the profits are taxable. It is the same with any item.

Note that it is *intention* that is important. It does not matter how long you held the shares – it is your intention at the time of purchase. It could well be that you buy shares for long-term investment at 100c but the next day something happens (redundancy, illness) and you have to cash up. The fact that you have a profit after just one day is irrelevant; you did not buy them intending to sell them on at a profit and so the profit is tax free.

Intention can be difficult to prove, of course. At one end of the spectrum, someone who stags shares quite clearly is going to pay tax on the profits. However, there are people who buy shares and are not very clear on why they have bought them or when they will sell them – if they go up in value immediately they may take their profits, if they don't they may hold them for the dividend. As a matter of policy, the IRD will look for pointers such as a track record of buying and selling quickly, using margin trading facilities which are short-term borrowings, notes or material on the long-term prospects for the company (e.g. five-year forecasts), etc. Ultimately, the onus is on you to show what your intention was at the time of purchase. It pays to keep any notes or research that you have made. For example, a tip sheet may recommend a share as a good long-term investment – you should file the article with its recommendation.

Intention can be difficult to prove.

DOUBLE-EDGED SWORD

Of course, whether a particular share was purchased to trade or as a long-term investment can be a double-edged sword. Sometimes a share will go down in value and you will make a loss. Is that loss deductible against your other income (wages, business income, etc) or is it not? The answer again depends on whether it was a capital loss (non-deductible) or a trading loss (deductible). And this too comes down to your intention – if you are intending to trade shares, any losses can be deducted against other income; if you are intending to hold them as a long-term investment, the loss is not deductible.

	PROFITS	LOSSES
Trader	taxable	tax deductible
Investor	tax free	non-deductible

You can be both trader and investor. Just because you have been a trader on one set of transactions does not mean that you are a trader on all of your sharemarket operations.

> You can be both trader and investor.

The law says that it is your intention and purpose at the time of making any particular purchase. You can therefore trade one group of shares but invest in another. The tax treatment for the two portfolios is different. This was well illustrated by the affairs of someone I know. For several years, from 1979 until 1987, this individual invested in shares and built up a substantial portfolio. He made occasional alterations and adjustments but there was no question that this was an investment portfolio. In 1986, with the markets booming, he decided to cease work and stay at home trading shares. He borrowed some money short term and opened a couple of margin trading facilities, and in early 1987 started to buy shares. He kept his investment portfolio separate.

The trading portfolio went badly. 'Badly' turned to 'disastrously' on 20 October 1987 when the market crashed. Our trader/investor recognised that the world had changed and sold everything, investments and trading stock, on that day and a day or two later. By the end of that week he was completely out of the sharemarket.

His profit-and-loss situation was interesting. He had losses on his trading portfolio, but because he had been investing so long his investment shares were sold at a profit. His situation was this:

Investment portfolio	profit	+$110,000
Trading portfolio	loss	-$ 30,000

Come tax time, he decided to claim the $30,000 loss against his other income. Before the IRD wrote a cheque for the tax refund, it decided to have a look at the total situation. When it saw the investment 'profit' of $110,000 it quite predictably decided that the investor/trader could not have it both ways.

However, the investor/trader decided to fight the IRD. He could easily show that the investment portfolio was just that and quite quickly gained acceptance that this was not taxable profit. He then wrote the IRD a long letter to show that in late 1986 he had gone into the business of share trading. He could prove this because:

- he had always kept the trading portfolio separate.
- he funded his short-term trading with short-term borrowings, evidence that he did not intend to hold the shares long term.
- he had sold his previous business and so his only expected income was now to come from share trading.
- he had installed a computer with on-line capabilities (a very early model) so that he could get up-to-the minute share price information.

Eventually the IRD accepted his case – he capitalised his profits and deducted his losses. He could indeed have it both ways!

While that investor got his timing wrong (he was in good company!) the idea was a valid one. You don't have to give up work or sell your business: even without doing that you can still run a long-term investment portfolio (which will make you most of your money) and a trading operation which might make you a bit of money but will certainly give some fun and excitement. The tax treatment of each operation is quite different, providing you can show your intention for each purchase.

A SECOND ENTITY

What may help in this is to run the trading shares and the investment portfolio through different entities. That means having one of the activities owned and operated by a company while the other is in your personal ownership. For example, John Smith might own a portfolio of shares for long-term investment purposes while a company or a family trust (John Smith Ltd or The John Smith Family Trust) carries on the business of trading shares.

Although this means having another entity to manage and do tax returns for, it has the effect of separating the activities further and clearly showing the intention of each one. Each is a separate tax entity with its own IRD number and its own activity. This may make it easier for you to keep the activities separate as well as clearly showing that there are two separate activities in quite different entities.

DIVIDENDS

This is the second form of profits from shares. The bad news is that dividends are all taxable in the hands of the recipient shareholder. The good news is that they have usually been taxed already and, assuming that the company in which you have invested has paid tax at 30 cents on its profits, you will have little or no further tax to pay. This is because of the imputation system.

THE IMPUTATION SYSTEM

Imputations were brought in to alleviate the very unfair double taxation of dividends. What happened was that a company made profits and was taxed on those profits at the company tax rate. Some of these tax-paid profits were paid out to shareholders as dividends. The dividend was then taxed again in the shareholders' hands at each shareholder's personal rate. This resulted in double taxation.

The imputation system gives a tax credit on dividends from companies that have already paid tax on their profits. The credit is to the amount or percentage of tax that the company has paid.

This is usually 30 cents in the dollar. Note, however, that it is only if the company has paid tax in New Zealand that an imputation credit results. If you have invested in companies that pay tax offshore, you will have to pay tax on the amount of the dividend received even though the company has already paid tax on its profits. You get no credit for the tax that the company has paid in the foreign country. In this case, Australia is considered a foreign country although there are government talks going on at the moment to make imputation credits (the Australians call them franking credits) apply to both countries.

Assume that your company is paying tax on its profits at 30 cents (as most do) and pays a dividend of 10 cents per share (cps) out of that tax-paid profit and that you are on a tax rate of 38 cents. That company would pay a net dividend to you of 7 cps:

Dividend received	7 cps
Imputation credit	3 cps
Gross income	10 cps
Tax on 10 cps (assuming 38%)	3.8 cps
Less imputation	3 cps
Tax payable	0.8 cps

PROBLEMS FOR HIGH INCOME EARNERS

All personal income over $70,000 pa is taxed at 38 cents. Because companies never pay more than 30 cents this is the maximum amount of the imputation credit. If you are on the top marginal tax rate of 38 cents you will have to pay tax on the difference – the dividend that you receive is taxed at 38 cents. You have to make up the difference. This is also relevant to lower income earners who have invested in companies that pay lower rates of tax. The company might be on a lower rate of tax because it has tax losses it is using from previous years. If the company is paying tax at 10 cents and you are on 21 cents, you will again have to pay the difference. Although this is relatively rare, it does happen and makes such companies less attractive as investments.

SOLUTIONS FOR HIGH INCOME EARNERS

The way to avoid paying the extra tax on dividends is to own your shares through a company. Companies pay tax on income at a flat rate of 30 cents. If your personal company holds the shares, it will receive the dividends because it is the shareholder. Assuming the company that you are invested in is paying tax at 30 cents, your company or trust is on a tax rate which matches that and so the imputation credits will mean no more tax to pay. You may have substantial other income which means that you are paying tax at the top marginal rate of 38 cents; however, at least the dividends from your investments are taxed at only 30 cents.

Forming a company to hold your investments does, however, have disadvantages. It is another entity to manage, to do accounts for and, in the case of a company, an annual return has to be filed. All of this is inconvenient and costs. You want to make sure that you will have a significant tax saving (at least $500 each year) before you do it.

Tax can be a major cost of investing. It can nibble, bite, even chomp into your returns. It pays to know the rules and structure your affairs accordingly. If you are ever in doubt regarding the taxation of your investment, you should consult a tax adviser or an accountant. That might cost a bit, but your accountant ought to be able to save you in tax and trouble to at least the amount of their fees.

> The way to avoid paying the extra tax on dividends is to own your shares through a company or a family trust.

PART 2

Beat the market

INTRODUCTION

You can beat the market

Everyone can decide to beat the average almost regardless of the pursuit. Whether it is scholastic achievement, cooking, public speaking, rock climbing or share trading, everyone can aspire to be above average. However (and here's the bad news!), to do so usually means work and application. Only the very talented succeed without putting in effort – and think how much more successful they would be with some application. Smart investors, like smart cooks, smart rock climbers, and smart scholars, resolve at the start to put in the work. That resolution is probably the best decision they will ever make.

Nowhere is this more true than with buying and selling shares. Natural talent in this activity hardly rates at all. What does rate is focus, discipline, planning, organisation, analysis and work. None of these sound very attractive. Shares are not a lazy way to riches. I am sorry for that – I am no great fan of the Calvinist work ethic for its own sake. However, I know of no share system that will help you to beat the market that does not require some work. If you are not going to put in the effort, if you are not going to be organised and disciplined, you should 'buy the index' and be content with being average.

I know of no share system that will help you to beat the market that does not require some work.

Many people see the sharemarket as a great gamble, believing it to be little more than a rich man's casino. I do not believe that to be true – there is little luck in succeeding or failing with shares. It is certainly true that there are risks in investing in shares. In fact, there are risks in all investment types: to invest you must give your money to someone else and as soon as you do that there is always going to be a chance that you won't get it back again. However, all of the chance and much of the risk can be removed: by analysing, by thinking, by planning, by consistent application of a strategy, by knowing the markets and what you are getting into – and by always being in a position to seize an opportunity. You cannot remove the risk of short-term downside, but you can remove much of the risk of long-term failure.

You cannot remove the risk of short-term downside, but you can remove much of the risk of long-term failure.

NOTHING GOOD IS EASY

The top performers do not beat the market through tips from their mates – they do so by searching for value and understanding the economy, the markets and their companies. Nothing good is ever going to be easy.

However, the good news is that the skills and strategies that you can learn to beat the average are not just for now nor just for this market. These are things that you can use for ever. Too many people think only of the moment. When they miss an opportunity (say, Ryman or Google) they curse, and then turn their backs on the market. Instead of seeking out the next Ryman or the next Google, they curse their 'luck' – and do nothing. In fact, regardless of what has gone on before, regardless of any previous great bull runs, there are always new opportunities. You may miss one opportunity, but be assured there are others not far away.

Much the same happens when investors make mistakes. A 'dabble' in the market (from a tip from a family member) leads to a loss. That loss puts the investor off shares for good – not just investing with a 'dabble' but even going into a broadly diversified portfolio or managed share fund, let alone a serious sharemarket strategy for wealth. That's a great pity because no long-term saver or investor can afford to ignore the sharemarket. There is nothing surer than if you invest in shares for a while you will make mistakes. These mistakes will lead to losses – although not always: some mistakes arise from not investing, rather than buying the wrong thing. You can choose what you learn from your mistakes. You can learn that you do not want anything more to do with shares again, ever . . . or you can look at what you did wrong and make sure that you do not make the same mistake again (or any other mistake similar to it). The key is to make sure that the mistakes that you will inevitably make are not too damaging.

There is nothing surer than if you invest in shares for a while you will make mistakes.

CONTROL YOUR AGGRESSION

In the early days of your sharemarket career, make sure that you are not too aggressive. Have most of your funds spread across a range of companies with only a small proportion in companies in which you have taken a strong position. You may have 80% of your money in a passive index tracker (which will perform roughly at the average) and 20% in two or three companies you think will outperform. As you gain more experience and ability, you can be more aggressive and move money out of the index tracker and into companies that you think will do better than average. Make haste slowly – those inevitable mistakes will surely be painful; make sure that they are not fatal.

There is no such thing as a foolproof share trading or investment system that works every time. I've been in the sharemarket for 30 years but I've never come across a 100% accurate way of predicting future prices (if I ever did, I wouldn't write about it!). However, there are ways to minimise risk and mistakes. Much of people's success comes from looking after the downside first, buying into shares which may not perform spectacularly but which have a limited chance of loss. This is a safety-first approach, and it is right for all but the very best operators. It can take a long time to get back to your start point if a substantial part of your portfolio has been wiped out.

SHORT TERM OR LONG TERM

The sharemarket is a good medium for both long-term investment and short-term trading. Most of us do both, fitting on the spectrum where we are most comfortable. There is a risk in trying to beat the market – if you stick your neck out beyond the index it just might get cut off. However, with work and discipline and the application of a sensible strategy you can do it, and do it consistently.

Of course with shares, the average itself is pretty good. Over a 10-year period shares usually give good returns. As long as you don't take a time period around one of the periodic dislocations or crashes, you will find that shares consistently beat bank deposits or bonds and will often outperform property.

You will find that shares consistently beat bank deposits or bonds and will often outperform property.

Of course, when you look at such historical performances, you are almost always comparing averages. However, the aim of this book is for you to perform better than average, to beat the market and the majority of players in it.

Contrary to the belief of some people, this is not impossible. If there is an average performance (and there is – it is represented by the index), it stands to reason that some people will be above average while some people will be below. While there are those who are quite content to be average, there are others who would never be satisfied with that.

THE AVERAGE

With shares, the average is measured by use of an index. An index is made up of a basket of shares in a certain proportion. Once the shares are selected to go into the index in a particular proportion, the index will move up or down as the individual shares move in value. Most importantly, perhaps, the index will act as a benchmark, something with which to compare your own performance.

There are lots of different indices, though the best known and most used in New Zealand is the NZX50 index. This index is made up of the 50 biggest companies that are listed on the New Zealand Stock Exchange. The shares are put into the index and are weighted in proportion to the size of the companies. In this case, 'company size' is market capitalisation – the total number of shares on issue multiplied by the share price. The market capitalisation is the total value that the company is worth, the value of all of its shares – in other words, it would be what you would have to pay to buy the entire company.

At the time of writing, the NZX50 started with Fletcher Building, which made up 13.26% of the index:

1.	Fletcher Building	13.26%
2.	Telecom	12.12%
3	Contact Energy	9.22%
4	Auckland Airport	6.45%
5.	Sky City	4.99%
6.	F & P Healthcare	4.6%

and went down to some of the minnows:

47.	Hallenstein Glassons	0.31%
48.	Restaurant Brands	0.27%
49.	Cavalier	0.2%
50.	NZ Farming Systems	0.1%

You can imagine this as a share portfolio of which 13.26% is made up of Fletcher Building shares and 6.45% is made up of Auckland

International Airport, etc. Each has a weighting according to its size – Telecom makes up 12.12% of the portfolio, Cavalier 0.2%. If you think of this index as your own share portfolio, you would quickly see that the performance of just a few shares would dominate the performance of the portfolio. What the share price of Fletcher Building does will affect the overall value of the index far more than any ups or downs of Hallenstein Glassons. This synthetic share portfolio (the index) has 12.12% of its money in Telecom and only 0.27% in Restaurant Brands.

This is only one index – there are lots of others. There is the NZX10 (the top 10 companies), Small Companies Index, technology index, world indices, etc. If you go to the USA you will find a transport index, healthcare index, tobacco index, energy index – all of which provide a benchmark for investment performance in a particular area. These are synthetic share portfolios, created to provide a benchmark which gives an average measure of performance within their particular industry. If you were interested in investing in healthcare, for example, you could measure your performance in that area by looking at the healthcare index.

CAPITAL OR GROSS INDEX

All indices represent a basket of shares. However, you need to be careful when looking at them because they can be measuring different things. Some indices are measuring the gross returns from the shares in the index (i.e. returns from both capital gains and dividends). A *gross* index gives a measurement of returns as if all dividends had been reinvested back into the shares. A capital index, however, represents only the capital gains or losses from the shares. It is as if the dividends were all taken out and spent. Clearly there is a great deal of difference in value if dividends are accumulated with the shares in the index or if the index is solely measuring share price movements.

The NZX50 is a gross index – it includes dividends and treats them as if they have been reinvested. The NZX50 is the most widely used measure of average and has largely taken over from the NZSE40, which was a capital index. As such, the NZX50 will certainly outperform the old NZSE40.

HOW TO BE AVERAGE

In some activities it is fine to be average: some people have to work hard to be an average golfer, some have to work hard to get 50% in an exam. With shares, it is also okay to be average – you will still make good money (just as an average golfer still enjoys the game). However, although the average is quite satisfactory for shares, you do not have to work hard to achieve it – it is simplicity itself.

To achieve the average, you could:

1. Buy all of the shares that are in the index in the right proportion. This would be a fairly big exercise – to match the NZX50 perfectly, you would have to own 50 different companies and put up with all of the administration that this would entail. In fact if you bought the top 8 or 10 companies in the index the performance of that portfolio would likely be fairly close to the index because the big companies dominate and effectively drive the index.

2. You could buy an 'index tracker'. These are passive managed funds which deliberately set out to match (or track) the index. Unlike actively managed funds where the manager selects shares and buys and sells them routinely, the capital profits of the index trackers are not taxable – a considerable advantage. Given that an index tracker has a portfolio that matches a particular index, its performance will equate to the index, less a little bit for fees. Because the portfolio requires no analysis or stock picking, the fees for managing an index tracking fund are quite small. The NZX offers a range of index funds under the brand 'Smartshares': the best known are TENZ (which tracks the top 10 New Zealand companies) and FONZ (which tracks the top 50 shares). Another well-known index tracker is WiNZ

(which tracks the world index), and there are many others offered by fund managers.

AVERAGE IS FOR WIMPS?

No it's not. Aiming to be an average investor works for a lot of people. Large numbers of people will be very satisfied with a return which equates to the average. Beating the market is not for everyone.

Aiming to match the index is for people who:

- Lack time to concentrate on their share investments. Beating the market doesn't just happen – it needs work.
- Lack skills and interest. There are many people who have money to invest but are really not very interested in actively managing their money and perhaps know that they are not very good at investing. An average return from shares is just fine with them.

> Beating the market is not for everyone.

- Have little appetite for risk. Being better than average means taking some risks. To beat the market you must move outside the index and start to pick winners. That requires thinking and analysing and then putting your money where your analysis is. Sometimes you will get things wrong.
- Beginning investors. Those who are just starting out in share investment will want to stay fairly close to the average, not pushing too far until they have more skill and experience. As someone just learning about the sharemarket, an average performance is just fine.

> To beat the market you must move outside the index and start to pick winners.

Any of these groups should be happy with an average return from their share investments and either buy an index tracker or stay with a few of the heavyweight companies. Alternatively they might buy into one of the dozens of actively managed unit trusts that are available. The managers of these try hard to beat the index and, after fees and tax, some succeed while others don't.

BETTER THAN AVERAGE

Others will want to try to beat the market – some will want to beat it by a lot and try for an annual return of 25% or more, while some will only want to slightly enhance their returns. The more you try to beat the market, the more you must stick your neck out.

To be better than average, to beat the market, you must move away from the mainstream and what is in the index. That means doing one of the following:

1. Buying shares that are not in the index, often because the companies are too small. Very often smaller companies do better as investments than bigger, more mature ones. Smaller companies generally do better than bigger ones – but carry more risk.

2. Buying only a small number of companies. The more companies that you have, the greater your diversification and therefore the less volatility or risk. Holding only a few companies will mean higher risk but a greater chance of out-performance.

3. Buying shares in a company in a higher proportion than its weighting in the index. For example, Fletcher Building might be in the index at 13.26%. If you have 50% of your portfolio in Fletcher Building, you will tend to either outperform or underperform the index according to what Fletcher Building does.

To do any of these is to back yourself (with your money) to choose well. Moving outside of following the index means that you might beat the average – it also means that the average might beat you. This is why for many people index tracking is such a sane thing to do. Index tracking to be average may

> **Try to beat the market only if you are sure you can do it.**

seem wimpish but there is often only a small difference between courage and stupidity. Try to beat the market only if you are sure you can do it. Otherwise you are wise to let discretion be the better part of valour.

THE WINNING MARGIN

The extent to which you try to beat the market is a matter of choice. There is a spectrum which on the one side would see someone moving away from the index with only a little of their available money. Someone at the other end of the spectrum might be far more aggressive and try to beat the market by a long way.

This spectrum ranges from the defensive investor who will hold most of the bigger companies in the NZX50 (or perhaps an index tracker) spread across a range of industries, to an aggressive investor who holds perhaps only four or five companies which are smaller but will be well analysed. The aggressive investor is carefully picking stocks with the confidence that comes from experience. Certainly aggressive investors are taking greater risks but that risk is mitigated by the investment skills that they have.

Defensive unskilled investor	Aggressive skilled investor
←	→
• many, large companies	• few, smaller companies
• several different industries	• only one or two industries
• low risk	• high risk

For example, take someone with $50,000 to invest:

Aggressive investor's portfolio:

Ryman	$ 15,000
Kathmandu	$ 5000
Rakon	$ 15,000
GPG	$ 10,000
Fletcher Building	$ 5000
	$ 50,000

Defensive investor's portfolio:

TENZ (index tracker)	$ 40,000
GPG	$ 5000
Michael Hill	$ 5000
	$ 50,000

Clearly the defensive investor is going to perform only a little differently from the market. He or she has decided mainly to match the index and hopes only to outperform by a small amount. Because of the holding of an index tracker (in this case TENZ) the investor has considerably more diversification than the aggressive investor. The risk of losses to the portfolio is lower as is the risk of the sharemarket overall moving ahead but leaving the investor behind. The more aggressive investor might get great returns (if the choices are right) but might also be sidelined.

A GOOD PLACE TO START

Nevertheless, the defensive portfolio is a good way for many people to start off in the market. Having most of their money in an index tracker (or if desired, a number of the market heavyweights) with only a small amount of money in smaller companies cuts risk at a time when the investor is most vulnerable – that is, when the investor is inexperienced.

Shares are too important an investment to ignore. It is no excuse for failing to invest to claim inexperience or lack of skill. This is something that does not require a blind plunge into the deep end of the pool. It is something that can be learnt gradually, where the stakes need to be increased only when you are ready.

THE COMPETITION

If the index represents an average performance, it is obvious that some people will be above it while some will be below it. To beat the market, you are really looking to beat the other players in the market – or at least most of them.

Think about your biggest competition, the others who are

investing in the sharemarket. While large numbers of these are small private investors like yourself (around 25% of the market is owned by New Zealand retail investors), the most significant part of the money in the market comes from institutional and corporate investors. These may be from New Zealand or may be offshore investors. Most of them are not investing their own money – they are fund managers (banks, insurance companies, superannuation funds) investing on behalf of others.

These are your biggest competition in the sharemarket. They do have advantages in the game – but so too do you.

ADVANTAGES OF INSTITUTIONAL INVESTORS

- They are disciplined – generally they have a system and guidelines and they stick to them.
- They are full-time investors – they spend all day, every day, striving for better returns.
- They are well connected and well informed – they are likely to pick up rumours very quickly.
- They are dispassionate and have no emotional attachment to what is happening.
- They are able to make company visits. The CEO of a listed company would be only too happy to discuss the company's prospects with a large institution but will not open the books for you with your 2,000 shares.

However, small investors do have some advantages over the big institutions.

ADVANTAGES OF PRIVATE INVESTORS

- You can move quickly and easily into and out of the market. Selling $20,000 of shares can usually be done immediately – selling $20 million of shares may take some time. Those $20 million of shares that an institution wants to sell will probably in themselves depress the share price – your $20,000 worth is a mere ripple in the market.

- You can go into smaller companies. An institution has to buy a lot of shares for it to make a significant difference to the portfolio. Sometimes smaller companies simply do not have enough shares on issue to warrant institutional investment even though it is a high-performing company.
- You are investing your own money – you have every incentive to invest it well.
- You can buy what you want, risk what you want. No one is going to criticise you if you go heavily into a particular company and it doesn't work out. You have no need to look over your shoulder and worry about what your boss or your unit holders will think when you make a mistake.
- You do not have to continue to own shares in bad times. Many managed funds have a mandate which means they must be 100% invested at all times. You, on the other hand, can sell out for a time and watch from the sidelines.

Although the big institutions have advantages, you do also. You can beat them (and the rest of the market) – particularly if you learn from the institutions and adopt some of their advantages.

You can:

- Be dispassionate and unemotional about your investments, making your decisions by thinking rather than feeling.
- Be disciplined and work to predetermined, planned guidelines.
- Be well informed, develop a network of contacts, attend seminars, read investment literature, etc.

> **Be dispassionate and unemotional about your investments . . .**

In fact, these are essentials if you are going to beat the market. A planned, rational and disciplined approach with decisions based on good information must be your aim. It is those who respond on emotion to the issue of the day, who act like reef fish when a shadow passes overhead, without any thought or planning, who are the losers in the market. These opportunistic part-timers are the market's easy beats.

With the adoption of a plan, the discipline to work to it and with good information, you can be better than average and beat the market. You will certainly do better than many of the small private investors and, quite probably, better than a lot of the big institutions.

Remember always that for every buyer, there is a seller – someone with a contrary view. If you are buying, the person who is selling has reasons to do so. Only one of you can be right – time will prove it to have been either right to buy or right to sell. It can't be both.

To beat the market, you need to be right most of the time!

WAY ONE

Know the markets

A market, any market, is like an organised argument. On the one side are the people who think the market will rise; on the other side are those who think it will fall. These are the bulls and the bears of the sharemarket – each group has an opinion contrary to the other and, ultimately, only one can be right.

The bulls are the optimists who think the market will rise and therefore buy or hold shares. The bears are pessimists who think the market will fall and therefore want to sell and not hold shares. (The easy way to remember this is that the bulls toss the market up with their horns while the bears tear it down with their claws.) The two sides are involved in a never-ending debate. The winner at any point is established at some time in the future – if the bulls can make a compelling case they will have others join them and, because they outnumber the bears, the market will rise. If the bears win the debate, the market will fall.

At any minute of any trading day the bulls and the bears will be balanced. The market has to be at a level where there are both bulls and bears. If you do not have both buyers and sellers, you do not have a market. Therefore if there is a lack on either side, the market will move quickly to attract that side. If there are no buyers at a certain price, sellers have to lower their offer until a buyer is attracted; if

> **At any minute of any trading day the bulls and the bears will be balanced.**

there are no sellers for a share, buyers have to up their bid. To make a market, things have to be at a price level where both buyers and sellers are in play.

The sharemarket, as I have previously noted, is a market like any other – cabbages, meat or a Greek fish market. Both sides are yelling at each other about what they think the price should be, making their offers of produce for sale, bidding, and finally agreeing on value and doing a deal. In Greece, one assumes that the market for fish is conducted with great noise and, to an outsider, in great confusion. However, its underlying premise is that it is a place where buyers can meet sellers and argue the price of fish.

In the case of the sharemarket, the argument is held in quiet, genteel surroundings. In fact it is now held on-line – no one yells at anyone else, no one thumps the table, no one walks out in a huff. It is all done with a click of the mouse. This was not always the case – New Zealand used to have a market in each of the main centres where brokers would meet to buy and sell and, occasionally, yell excitedly at each other.

Brokers doing their trades from their offices on a screen is far more efficient and cheaper than what used to happen. On a day when something big was happening it was fun to go down to the exchange and watch, but those early markets did not work perfectly – buyers were sometimes not matched with sellers even though both existed. Today, all the buy and sell quotes are listed on the screen – all of the bulls meet all of the bears on a telephone line. That works far better, giving a much more honest market with no one missing out and everyone being informed of all of the buyers or sellers at any one time.

FEAR AND GREED

However, although the sharemarket now works quietly, efficiently and electronically, its players still get emotional. People still make most of their decisions on the basis of how they *feel* rather than what they *think*. The two predominant emotions are fear and greed. It is these emotions that explain the huge swings in markets, the sudden jumps either up or down. People are fearful of losses and take any small amount of negative information, whether it affects the underlying performance of those companies in which they are invested or not, as a signal to sell. At the same time people's greed makes them want to be buyers or at least to hold shares – they do not want to miss out. The chance of a profit makes people rush to buy if some piece of information newly learnt looks to improve the market's prospects. Market players are like reef fish – the slightest change leads to a great rush in one direction or the other.

Market players are like reef fish – the slightest change leads to a great rush in one direction or the other.

This emotion-driven behaviour is not something that you should buy into. Certainly you should feel some fear and some greed – and at most times the feeling of fear is more healthy than the feeling of greed. You should try to be more dispassionate than most market participants, recognising at all times that most people are behaving solely according to how they feel rather than how they think.

MARKETS OVERREACT

Markets almost always overreact. Emotions and the herd mentality are such that prices are frequently pushed substantially higher or lower than what anyone would think is reasonable. In the long term the market is always right; but in the short term it is often far from an accurate reflection of value. Understanding this is a key to beating the market. If you join the herd you will always travel where the herd travels. To be better than average you have to step outside, by yourself, and take a position.

Scary though this sounds, you need to back yourself to be right: it helps to know that there will be volatility, and more volatility than anyone ever really intended. If you understand what is causing this volatility and know that it is inevitable, it is easier to stand alone.

The volatility of the sharemarket, so frightening to many people, is often not driven by any genuine change in the prospects of the market. Only rarely does a new piece of information become known which has a true long-term effect on the profitability, performance or value of a business. The market, through emotions of fear and greed, may push the value of shares dramatically up or down, but the reality is that the true value of companies as measured by the prospects of the businesses that they own is unaffected.

ACCEPT VOLATILITY

> Most successful investors accept, even welcome, the volatility of the sharemarket.

Most successful investors accept, even welcome, the volatility of the sharemarket. They know that most market players scatter in panic when a shadow passes overhead. To beat the market you have to recognise that the shadow is usually caused by something which is harmless (a cloud or a seagull). Only seldom is that shadow caused by something which is truly threatening, the market's equivalent of a shark. Only seldom does something happen which will make a fundamental long-term difference to the business you are invested in. Certainly, there are sharks and you have to keep a watch for them, but there are a lot more clouds and seagulls.

Most genuinely adverse events creep up slowly, they do not suddenly appear. A higher than expected inflation figure or lower than expected growth in GDP do not greatly alter a business's prospects – the employees still go to work in the morning, keep on making and selling things, and the business continues to be profitable. A little bit of extra inflation might make the business's managers work a bit harder and might mean that the profits are a little lower than expected for a while. That hardly seems a cause to panic and dump shares in what is fundamentally a good company. And yet that is what so many investors do: a relatively minor piece of news sees shares fall across the board with little thought about how this occurrence will truly affect long-term business prospects. Note also that the reaction is often indiscriminate – all companies are affected, regardless of what they do or how they make money.

SHORT-TERM FEELERS AND LONG-TERM THINKERS

The people who drive this volatility are short-term feelers – they make their decisions on the basis of fear and greed, trading in shares as a commodity rather than thinking about the underlying value of the business that they own a part of. There probably are not many of these people – remember that the market is always finely balanced and it takes only a few people to push it firmly in one direction or the other. This sudden volatility gets the headlines as a few people choose to buy or sell. However, it is only a few people and they are pushing the market on the basis of an emotional madness, an irrationality which may be overly exuberant or blindly panicked. They may be able to point to something that has caused their buy or sell behaviour but in the overall scheme of things, and in the long run, what they point to is trivial.

Long-term thinkers learn to recognise what is a real threat to their investments and what is not. Smart investors have analysed their investments and know the businesses into which they have put their money. They do not stop their analysis once their money has gone in – they keep on doing it, using their analysis and understanding as a filter to work out what is a real threat and what is baseless hype. The question should always be: how will this event or piece of information affect the business that I own? They know that the greatest threat to a good business is much more likely to be the gradual erosion of a brand or people's buying habits slowly changing. A strike at one of the factories or a one-quarter profit downgrade are unlikely to make much difference.

If you cannot accept the short-term volatility of the sharemarket and back yourself to work out what is real and what is not, you should not try to beat the market. Instead you should invest through an equity unit trust or a passive index tracker. To beat the market you have to accept that there will be ups and downs, and be able to work out what is an important event and what is something that is exciting only to journalists and reef fish.

THE MARKET'S EASY BEATS

You should welcome the volatility because it creates a divide between those who will succeed and those who will thrash around like minnows. The short-term feelers who overreact are the market's easy beats. If you have the ability to analyse, the patience to wait and the discipline to stay focused on what is important, you will succeed. Remember always that you own a part of a business and it is only the performance of that business which is important. As long as the business can keep growing its profits, that performance will sooner or later be reflected in the value of its shares. The smaller downward movement caused by scattering reef fish is really only another opportunity to buy into good businesses at cheap prices. If the reef fish want to give away good businesses because of their blind fear and panic, you should be prepared to take those businesses off their hands.

Nevertheless, it is never easy, even for the most disciplined and organised investor, to completely block out emotion and the noise of the market. I have always found it much easier to write 'buy in gloom, sell in boom' than to actually do it. Filtering out all of the comment (a mild word which does not really describe the hysteria that sometimes surrounds the market) requires not just focus and concentration but also a plan that has been made at a quiet time. The plan strains out the rubbish but lets the good stuff through.

> . . . it is only the performance of that business which is important.

Recognise, accept, even welcome the market's volatility – and profit from it. Decide now to be a thinker and to take advantage of those who operate only on the emotions of fear and greed. Set a clear strategy and follow it, rather than react to some happening which might seem of great significance at the time but in the bigger picture and over the long haul has little bearing on the business that you own a part of. Be prepared to stand alone, letting the reef fish go where they want.

YOU CAN'T BE A BULL AND A BEAR

In the final analysis you have to decide whether you like a share, are a bull and buy it, or dislike it, are a bear and sell it. There is no in between. The advice that some sharebrokers and tipsters give to 'hold' a share is often given as a sort of halfway house – the share is not rated as a 'buy' nor as a 'sell'. This is silly. To hold a share is to believe that it is going to do well – why else would you own it? If you hold a share you are a bull – you could sell nearly as easily as you can hold (one call to a broker). You need to be decisive – you are either a buyer or a seller, you are either in or you are out.

PROS AND CONS

Investment in shares requires decision-making. This is almost never straightforward because for the market to exist there needs to be both buyers and sellers. Each of these groups has their reasons, each side has some justification for what they are doing. Ultimately only one can prove to be right.

In all decision-making, I always find it best to commit both sides of the argument to paper. Decisions on buying or selling shares are no exception. Take a piece of blank paper and write 'pros' on one side and 'cons' on the other, and the list of all the factors under one heading or the other. This allows you to weigh the factors much more easily. It does not mean that you can make the decision by numbers – just because there are more 'pros' than 'cons' does not necessarily make it a good idea. However, it does allow you to see at a glance the important factors, and quite often when these factors are set out on paper it becomes obvious which side weighs the most.

A good example of this was when I was considering buying Telecom shares in June 2000. The past financial performance of Telecom had been excellent, but it seemed at a crossroads.

Invest in Telecom?

Pros	Cons
• Dominant NZ brand	• Management changes
• Growth expected from mobile and Xtra	• Possible regulation
• AAPT purchase – good long term?	• Recent profit weakness
• Possible spin-off of Xtra and mobile businesses into separately listed companies	• Increasing competition
	• Wireless Internet access from competitors
	• Dominance mainly in mature markets
	• Vodafone marketing aggressively

The cons seemed to be great enough to outweigh the pros and at the very least put enough doubt in my mind to stay out. This proved to be a good decision as the shares have fallen from 770c to as low as 400c in the time since.

Jotting down the pros and the cons like this forces you to look at both sides of the equation. It makes you at least consider the other side's position – the other side may be buying or selling on some short-term emotion but there might be other more substantial reasons. Putting the pros and cons in writing makes you think and gives the added advantage of giving you a record of your decision-making process. I seldom have trouble making a decision if I commit all of the factors to paper.

GIVE ME THREE GOOD REASONS

Another good check to see if what you are doing is the right thing is to ask yourself for three good reasons why you should sell a share (if you are thinking of buying it) or three good reasons why you should buy it (if you are going to sell it). If you don't like the implications involved in talking to yourself, you could get your spouse, a colleague or a sharemarket contact to ask for three good reasons for the contrary

> If a market is an organised argument, you need to know all sides of the question.

opinion, and then you can make your contrary case and try to convince them. If you can't come up with any compelling reasons for the view contrary to your own you could ring your brokers and get them to give three good reasons.

All of this provides a discipline in forcing you to look at *all* of the relevant factors. If a market is an organised argument, you need to know all sides of the question and be sure that you are debating from the right side.

THE MARKETS

There is more to consider than simply the market of the particular shares that you are interested in. Your shares trade in a wider environment and their performance is affected by that environment. It is useful to think of your shares within three markets:

1. The economy – the overall sharemarket.
2. The industry – the market for shares within a particular industry.
3. The company – the individual share that you are interested in.

Each of these works as a market, with information coming in and people acting and reacting, and often overreacting on the basis of it. The value of your investments will depend on each one and you need, therefore, to be continually analysing them all. However, as in any market, some of the information will be more important than other information and the players within each will overreact, pushing the market too far.

It is useful to see these three as a triangle:

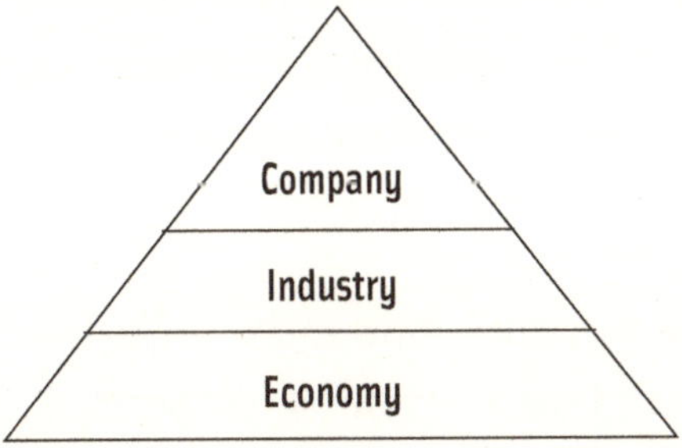

The economy that you invest in is the foundation – it is the environment for the performance of industries and your companies. If that environment is good, companies will find it easier to make money and perform. It is difficult for an industry to perform well in a poor economy and difficult for a company to perform well in a poor industry (especially if it is also in a poor economy). Company directors and managers have to be smart to grow their business in a poor environment (and think how much better they would do it if their economy and industry were booming).

However, it might be difficult, but it is by no means impossible. There are plenty of instances of good investments even when there is a poor economic and industry environment. Some years ago Baycorp and Port of Tauranga were both very good investments against the background of a poorly performing New Zealand economy. The Warehouse has also traded well only in the ordinary New Zealand economy, but its business and share price performed (until it went into Australia!). Conversely, while the New Zealand economy has been strong, there are nevertheless plenty of examples of companies that have not performed well. Most boats rise when the tide comes in – most are beached when it goes out. However, there are always a few that manage to sail away, finding deep water and a good wind, just as there are some that get grounded even when the tide is high.

This is why you cannot completely ignore investments simply because they are in a particular economy or industry. It is also why you should take all of the economic and industry comment with a grain of salt. There is money to be made even in an economy that is gloomy and depressed, provided you do not simply follow the reef fish.

> **There is money to be made even in an economy that is gloomy and depressed.**

CHOICES

You can choose which economy to invest in, which industry and which share. This is obvious in the case of the latter two, and more and more people are also making a deliberate choice in terms of which economy. Now it is quite easy to invest in the country and economy of your choice, be it Korea, USA, Canada, India, China, Ireland or UK, if you think that their economies will outperform. The choice is no longer simply to put your money into New Zealand companies. You can if you want go into the global economy – they are all interconnected now. If you simply want exposure to the world market you can buy WiNZ, an index tracker following the World Index.

Having said that and shown clearly elsewhere in this book that I believe New Zealanders should invest offshore, I do not think that all of your investments should be outside of this country. New Zealand is where you live. Certainly New Zealand's economy has been relatively poor over the last two or three decades. We have never really recovered from Britain joining the EC and from the oil shocks in the 1970s (at which time we made some bad calls). However, it is not that bad – we have had at least five good years and although we have just had a long recession, there are some good reasons to be positive about New Zealand's future. Moreover, there is a comfort in buying shares in companies that you know; companies that you perhaps deal with every day. I think investing in New Zealand makes sense because as New Zealanders we understand better what the companies that we own do, and have a good idea of how they are doing (you may shop at The Warehouse or Michael Hill, fly in or out of Auckland Airport or buy your electricity from Trust Power). In any event, you live here and need a natural hedge against it outperforming other economies over long periods of time. Given that this is where you live, you need a substantial part (if not a majority) of your investments here at home. Depending upon your circumstances, you should probably keep 40–60% of your investments in this country.

Many people choose the country that they want to invest in first, then decide on which industry and then look at the companies within that industry. Although this approach sounds quite neat and tidy, I think it is flawed. It would mean that investors would have had nothing in the New Zealand economy up until a couple of years ago (tell that to the shareholders of Ryman Healthcare). There are good companies making good profits in all countries and in all industries.

Nevertheless, it is easier to make good investments in economies and industries that are having a good time. At the very least, what happens in the economies and industries in which you are invested will affect the shares that you own. You therefore need to know what these influences are.

ECONOMY

There are two things which make watching and analysing the economy difficult. The first is that you are not wanting to assess the economy as it is, but how it is going to be. All investment is for the future – you are not investing in past performance. Therefore you are really wanting to make economic forecasts. This is extraordinarily difficult as economists prove every day.

The second difficulty is the political nature of economics and the way that the economy is 'improved' by politicians. All politicians want the same sort of economy: robust, strong and growing. However, their ideas of how to get that sort of environment differ markedly. Their economic moves depend upon their political colours. This can (and does) see lurches one way or the other as different politicians get their hands on the controls.

Confusing these two factors, politics and the difficulty in economic forecasting, is the fact that many of the people who talk about the state of the economy, where it is going and what should be done, have their own agendas and prejudices. Even some of the so-called independent economists, whether from banks or economic consultancy firms, speak from a platform that resembles a soap-box. It is easy enough to name individual economists on the tinder-dry right and economists on the soppy left. I am not sure that any of them can be trusted very far.

Nevertheless, the economy and its future direction is important to investors. Interestingly (and creating yet another difficulty for investors), the sharemarket will often lead the economy by 6–12 months. That is, the sharemarket will often start to move upwards months before the economy starts to recover from a recession or start to fall well before a strong period of economic growth runs out of steam. The smart money in the sharemarket knows what is happening in the economy before it happens! The smart money knows the direction of the economy better than the smart economist. Similarly, the sharemarket provides an accurate barometer for what is happening in the country's politics. The sharemarket has always seemed a far better place to read who is going to win an election than the most sophisticated opinion polls. The sharemarket is very sensitive to any change (including political change) and its performance in the run-up to an election speaks volumes on who will win and what investors think about the likely winner.

There are six main things to watch for in the economic environment:

- **Growth.** An economy which is expanding, rather than contracting, presents an easy time to make money. Profits are higher and these profits are announced in the annual (or half-year or quarterly) results. Economies are always cyclical – growth is followed by recession and vice versa. A period of strong and sustained growth, particularly if it is export-led, is very good for the sharemarket.

- **Interest rates.** High interest rates and rising interest rates are generally very negative for the sharemarket, while lower rates are very positive. This is for two reasons. First, most companies that are listed on the sharemarket have bank debt. If rates are low, their interest expense is low and so their profits will be higher. Second, the differing investment classes compete amongst themselves for the investor's dollar. If rates are low, investors will take money out of bank deposits and out of bonds and put it in the sharemarket or into property. This is especially so at times when dividend yields are higher than deposits or bonds and so people are attracted by the higher cash returns obtainable from a basket of shares.

- **Inflation.** Although inflation has now virtually been outlawed in New Zealand, it remains a worry, especially currently when the Government is running a large deficit. High inflation is generally negative for the sharemarket, low inflation is positive (although there are some famous exceptions to this rule). High inflation pushes up interest rates with negative effect (see above) as well as making the economy less competitive against the rest of the world.

- **Exchange rates.** Generally, a lower exchange rate is better for the economy. This is because New Zealand is a trading nation and dependent on exports. A low exchange rate makes exporting easier and helps the economy to grow, even though it may adversely affect some individual companies (e.g. The Warehouse, which imports a lot of its stock).

- **Liquidity.** This refers to the amount of money that is available to go into the market. There are times when there is a lot of money available to be invested in the sharemarket. It may come from high salaries or business profits during buoyant times, or from easy borrowings through banks or heavy promotion of margin trading facilities. Around the world markets soared partly because the baby boomer generation had become interested in investment and are now at an age where the children have left home, the mortgage has gone and, being at the top of their professions, they have high income. A large amount of this baby boomer investment money went into stockmarkets. A high level of takeover activity is very good for the market as this also increases liquidity. One company will buy out another company's shareholders who receive cash for their shares. At least some of this cash will find its way back into the market.

- **Political stability.** The economy and the market like political stability and hate uncertainty. Business can live with most rules as long as it knows what they are and they remain stable. The sharemarket does not usually like elections and will often perform badly in the lead-up to one (although it might start to move up if it likes the party that it has decided is going to win). Having said that, much movement in the sharemarket in New Zealand which is caused by political concerns is largely, in my view, irrational. There is not a great deal of difference between the philosophies and policies of the main parties and, regardless of who is in power, New Zealand will have reasonable political stability and no great anti-business policies.

Business can live with most rules as long as it knows what they are and they remain stable.

These six things form a matrix of economic and environmental factors which push the sharemarket. Each has its own effect – positive or negative.

	POSITIVE (BULLISH)	NEGATIVE (BEARISH)
Economic growth	high	low
Interest rates	low	high
Inflation	low	high
Exchange rate	low	high
Liquidity	high	low
Political stability	high	low

INDUSTRY

The industry that your investments are in is the second important factor. You need to assess which industries are likely to grow and which are likely to decline. Unfortunately, the New Zealand sharemarket does not give you much choice of industry type, the market being dominated by one big telecommunications company, some retail stocks, a bit of tourism and a collection of other bits and pieces. The real growth areas of our times (information technology and health) are hardly represented at all – you need to go offshore to go fully into these areas. Similarly, there is little available in resource stocks (gold, oil, nickel, etc) or in banking, although these industries are available on the Australian market. Nor does the New Zealand sharemarket have much representation of our biggest and best industry – agriculture.

> You want to choose sunrise industries rather than sunset industries.

Some industries wax while others wane – there are new industries coming onto the market every few years or so. It is always tempting to reject the old sunset industries for the newer more exciting sunrise industries. I don't think that people should put very much of their money into an industry early on in the sunrise – it pays to wait until there is a bit more than just a glimmer of light and the sun is properly above the horizon (I waited until 2005 before investing in Google). A company whose only asset and business is some research into a cure for AIDS is not deserving of a lot of your funds (I think I'd stay with an older industry like building rather than that). Many of the Internet stocks in the USA have withered and died to the cost of millions of investors. Investors should stay in industries (and with companies) that are already making profits. You might put a little money into something more speculative, but the bulk of funds should be in areas that have already proved that they can make profits.

THE COMPANY

Analysis of individual companies means looking at a whole range of things, some of which are covered elsewhere in this book. One thing that needs to be covered here is the idea that in many respects a company operating in a certain economy, in a particular industry, is really operating like a managed fund. With managed funds you choose the area that you want to invest in (say Asian equities or Australian commercial property), give your money to the fund manager and let them go to it.

Investing in a share is much the same. If you wanted to invest in Australasian telecommunications, you might choose to invest in Telecom. In effect you are giving your money to the directors and managers of Telecom and saying to them, go and invest and manage telecommunications businesses in Australasia. Alternatively, you might decide you want to invest in New Zealand tourism. If that is the economy and industry you want, you could give your money to Air New Zealand, Tourism Holdings, Sky City or Jasons and let them try to make money for you in your chosen area.

There is a lot more to choosing specific companies than this, of course: each company will have different plans, different assets and operate in different areas of the industry. However, viewing a company as a managed fund is useful because it forces you to take a wider view and think about the economy and industry it is operating in. It also forces you to think hard about that most important area of a company – its people and, especially, its management.

Only by knowing the three areas which influence the value of your investments (economy, industry and company) can you work out what is truly important to their long-term profitability. If you know these things you can swim safely in the opposite direction to the rest of the reef fish. Most players in the market are very reactive – you need to know enough to be able to take a contrary view when the situation warrants. Superior information and understanding is the key to beating most of the other players.

WAY TWO

Buy value

Smart investors keep half an eye on the market – but only half. Their full glare is directed at business trends, not market trends. Smart investors know that they are not buying a commodity called 'shares' on whose price they are speculating, but are instead buying a part of a business. The market interests them, but only in two respects:

1. Their short-term trading (perhaps 10–15% of their capital).
2. Their ability to buy into good businesses cheaply. In this respect a down market is often of greater interest than one which is up.

As far as top investors are concerned, the reef fish can largely do what they want. The sharemarket exists only to allow people to buy and sell bits of business. It is what is happening within those businesses that is of most interest.

There is an old saying with shares: buy quality shares, put them in the bottom drawer and forget them. While two-thirds of this strategy has much to commend it (it is about buying quality shares and holding on to shares for long periods of time), I don't think that you should forget them. Shares do need to be assessed and reassessed regularly to make sure that they still

> **Shares do need to be assessed and reassessed regularly to make sure that they still represent value.**

represent value. This is becoming even more true as businesses and industries are subject to continuous change.

It may have been possible in the past to put shares away and forget them but it certainly is not now. Industries come and go much more quickly. What used to be a great area in which to make money gets overtaken by events or technology. For example, meat processing used to be a certain way to make money – it is not something that I would quickly put money into now!

Industries and businesses have always come and gone. Now they come and go much faster. The pace of change and competition that can come from anywhere around the globe makes long-term success for businesses much more difficult. In business, the difference between great success and ruinous failure is now small. One wrong decision, one good move from a competitor, one invention that you don't have, can lead to a business being sidelined out of the game.

That means that you as an investor must watch the trends and be prepared to move. You can't just buy and forget. Michael Hill is a very good company right now – a good brand, good strategy and strong finances. However, it will only be a good investment while it stays ahead of the pack. It could easily miss a move and let someone else take its territory. Ride businesses like that while they hold their place. But if they ever falter, there is no room for sentimentality – sell them!

Nevertheless, there is no doubt in my mind that long-term investors will be more profitable than short-term traders. This is not to say that timing is not important or impossible. Nor does it exclude you from taking profits at times. It is just that owning good businesses is likely to be most profitable and that is where most of your money should go. Riding the long-term trends is likely to be better than trying to trade the short-term wrinkles. You do not want to simply buy and forget – but you do want to be in the market over long periods of time.

Long-term investing requires work. It requires business analysis skills which are at least good enough to understand the analysis of others (sharebrokers, tipsters, commentators, etc), if not good enough for you to research and analyse yourself. That work is ongoing. The analysis of the business does not simply happen before you buy into it but needs to be kept up throughout the ownership of shares in it. Note that I am not talking here of buying into the market overall; rather, I am talking about a selection of exceptional shares. You will probably want some exposure to the market's overall movement because shares on average are good investments. However, you should be aiming to do better than average, which means identifying and purchasing good businesses which will return perhaps 15% p.a. or more for years to you as owner. That is not average – that is exceptional. Nevertheless it is by no means impossible!

YOU ARE A BUSINESS OWNER

To do this requires good share selection and means approaching your task with the attitude of a prospective business owner. There is little difference between buying 100% of a small family business that you are going to run, or 0.001% of a large company. The amount and type of analysis is the same. That attitude of ownership is the foundation for the success of really smart investors.

There is a very useful discipline here: pretend that you are not about to buy a share in a business but instead are to buy the entire business. If you were to buy the whole lot, you would certainly do a very thorough due diligence before confirming a contract. You would understand the business, its assets, its brands, its prospects, its management and its people. Why should buying a share in it be any different? The principle is exactly the same, only the amount of money is different. Buying shares as if buying the entire business is precisely the right attitude for a successful investor.

> Pretend that you are not about to buy a share in a business but instead are to buy the entire business.

The sorts of things that anyone doing due diligence would look at are:

- Management
- Historic performance
- Brands and trademarks owned
- Quality of assets
- Budgets
- Earnings growth
- Threats
- Opportunities

MANAGEMENT IS CRUCIAL

When you buy some shares in a company it becomes your company and your business (albeit only in part). However, although it is now yours, you will not manage it. In fact your influence on direction and management is somewhere between negligible and non-existent. This is, of course, the major difference between buying 100% of a small family business and 0.00001% of Fletcher Building. You will manage the family business while Jonathan Ling manages Fletcher Building.

This discourages some independent-minded spirits from ever owning shares at all. These people tend to gravitate towards property or their own business where they believe that they have more control over their investment identity. Such people would no more put their money into shares than they would give it to a fund manager to look after in a unit trust.

In fact, it can be very useful to think of shares in a company as being very similar to managed funds. I know managing directors of listed companies who regard themselves as fund managers – they take the public money which goes into the company on the understanding that it will be invested in certain businesses and industries. In the case of Telecom, for example, the public gave its money to the company on the understanding that the directors and managers would use it to own telecommunications businesses.

However, although other people direct and manage the company, it is yours – your shareholding means that you are the company, you own it. You probably do not have much influence over it – 10,000 shares in Fletcher Building might be worth $75,000 and represent a lot of money to you, but it is only 0.002% of the company. That is not enough to have much say in the company's affairs. You could try ringing Mr Ling to tell him what you think he should be doing with your company, but you will probably not get far! Nevertheless, it is your company and your business, and you should make and hold your investment with that attitude. In the final analysis, a company is only a group of people (the shareholders) who have got together to make money from owning a business.

LOOKING FOR VALUE

When I talk about shares at seminars, I like to play a game. Right at the beginning I hold up my fountain pen (the one that I am writing this with) and ask for offers. The pen is a gold 'Cross', about eight years old, comes with a lifetime guarantee, works perfectly and retails at $600.

After a bit of a pause the offers come in. They usually range from 50c ('I could buy a biro for that and it would do the job') to $300 ('about half replacement').

I tell them that they are all miserable buggers and anyway the pen is not for sale (the person who gave it to me would kill me).

Then I give them some more information. I ask the audience to suspend disbelief and pretend that ownership of this pen would give them an income of $100,000 every year after all management costs for the foreseeable future. (The audience has to suspend disbelief because everyone knows that authors get paid a meagre pittance.)

Now things have changed. No longer is the audience bidding for a thing (or an asset) – instead they are bidding for an income stream. The most usual bid is $1m.

'Why?' I ask.

'Because I can get 6% at the bank but if I buy the pen I'll be getting 10%,' is the answer.

That's a very rational response. The audience knows that they have to get more income from the pen because of the risk (authors are a strange lot and could take off on an expedition to Mt Everest at any time). They need to get a better return to forsake the safety of a bank. Not only is the return better than an (almost) risk-free investment at the bank but also, at the back of the audience's mind, is the idea that the pen might write an international best-seller and therefore the income will grow dramatically. (Somehow I can't see the pen I am holding at the moment writing an international best-seller.)

THE SHAREMARKET IS THE SAME

The sharemarket is no different. It is an organised auction for ownership of an income stream. Instead of bidding for pens, the market is bidding for a share in a company and therefore a share in an income stream. That income stream is the company's profits. Just like the rational audiences that I speak to, the market will bid a price according to the risk that the profits might stop and according to its hope that they might grow. There is no reason why you would invest in anything even slightly risky if the return was not higher than what you could get at the bank, and every reason for you to invest if either the return was substantially higher and/or the return might grow.

Every minute of every day there are people making that assessment and then buying or selling according to their judgement. The best investors are in a continual search for value. They are not looking for investments with glamour or popular appeal or things which are 'in'. They are not looking for the next kiwifruit, deer, ostrich eggs, timeshare . . . the kinds of

> The best investors are in a continual search for value.

things that everyone talks about – the kinds of things which might boom for a while; then surely bust. Smart investors want value.

VALUE MEANS INCOME

In investment terms, value is about income. It is the income that can be obtained which both defines investments and gives them their value. Without income (or at least the prospect of income) you are not buying an investment at all – you are speculating on a price change that will be to your advantage. Investments have income which is completely separate from any change in price of the investment itself. It is the amount, growth and quality of the income that gives value to the investment. My gold pen has a value of 50 cents to $300 as it is. However, if it comes with an earnings stream of $100,000 p.a. my seminar audiences think it is worth $1m. The difference in value between $300 and $1m comes about solely due to its income.

With shares, the income comes from the company's profits. Sometimes that income is reasonably regular and continuous (e.g. infrastructure and utility companies like Trust Power or Contact Energy); sometimes it is slow and spasmodic (e.g. mining shares like NZ Oil and Gas); sometimes the income is prospective – that is, there is no income yet but plenty is expected (e.g. companies like NZ Farming Systems).

Whenever it comes, it is the prospect of cash profits which sets the value of any company. The assets that it owns are usually irrelevant – it is the profits that the company's management can wring from those assets that is important. Buying good shares is choosing companies that will make good profits. Nearly everything else regarding shares is simply a refinement of that idea – if you buy companies that do end up making good profits you will do well.

> It is the prospect of cash profits which sets the value of any company.

GOOD PROFITS

Successful sharemarket investment is about profits. However, there are profits and profits. Buying into the right company is not simply about choosing the one which makes the most profits – there are four other considerations.

1. **Are the profits sustainable?** This is what makes utility companies more attractive than some other trading concerns. Utilities (things like power and water) are regarded as being at least partially recession-proof. Like toilet paper, people keep using power and the telephone, even in economic hard times. Profits which are sustainable, which are less dependent on markets, exchange rates or management decisions are more desirable. The profits of Trust Power would be regarded as more sustainable than those of GPG (an investment company headed by Sir Ron Brierley which depends for a part of its profits on trading shares). Telecom would usually be rated higher than GPG by the market simply on the basis that its profits are more sustainable.

2. **When are the profits coming?** The most desirable company to buy into is one where the profits are already flowing – i.e. an established, profitable business. This is clearly more desirable than a start-up company in, say, wine, which is not expected to start making money for some years. This, of course, was the problem with many of the failed hi-tech stocks in the USA (especially the Internet ones) where even the most optimistic analysts did not predict positive cashflows for years, and the cash that the companies had was used before profits started to flow. The prospective profits might be huge – but they are only prospective. It is clearly more desirable to be in a company which has a track record of profitability.

3. **Are the profits in cash?** Some companies have very strong cash-flows. For example, Sky TV has cash income far in excess of its profits. Other companies find that their profits are to a large

extent tied up in working capital; things like stock or book debts – profits have to be retained in the business to keep it going and to fund new projects and cannot be paid out to shareholders. Sometimes 'profits' are unrealised gains on assets like property. Clearly, the quality of profits is important.

4. **Are the profits likely to grow?** If the profits increase, the value of the company's shares will increase too. This is much of the reason for the success of Ryman for its shareholders – growing profits have led to a higher and higher share price. The sharemarket will quickly push up the share price of a company if higher profits are expected – and just as quickly dump the share price if profits are likely to fall.

Much of the analysis of companies concerns ascertaining the health of the business and its likelihood of making money. Sharebrokers and some fund managers have something of an advantage in this respect because they can make company visits and query management on what is going on. We smaller private investors need to get much of our information at second hand.

ANALYSING A COMPANY

When you are analysing what you think is the value of the shares of a company, you are in effect valuing the company's business and then calculating how much each share in that business is worth. Business valuation is a fairly specialist activity and there can be a great range of numbers and ratios that can be looked at and compared with other businesses in the same industry. These are things like quick ratio, sales to EBIT (Earnings Before Interest and Tax) ratio, debtors to sales ratio, stock turn, etc, which will give indicators as to the health and prospects of the business. Most of them are for accountants and professional analysts, and probably are not necessary for smaller private investors. This is not to say that they are not important – however, most private investors will find it difficult to get complete information (this often comes from a company visit) and will therefore rely on the professional analysts in sharebroking firms.

What is important for the private investor, however, is the ability to review the company's annual reports and financial statements and to be able to read and understand analysts' reports. This requires a little financial skill and some common sense. The most important part of these statements is usually the notes to the accounts.

There are three main indicators of value. If you cannot understand these three things you should forget about investing yourself and instead rely on a fund manager. These three are the bare minimum:

1. Price:earnings ratio.
2. Dividend yield.
3. Net tangible asset backing.

PRICE:EARNINGS RATIO

The P:E ratio compares the amount of profits coming from the business to the price that you are going to pay for it. It is the same as the auction for my gold pen: once you know the amount of profits, then you have to decide how much you will pay for those profits. For sharemarket people, it compares the earnings which are attributable to each share with the share price. It is a concept that many stumble on. However, it is critical in assessing the value of shares; there is nothing more important than a company's P:E ratio.

Take a business that is making a tax-paid profit of $1m each year. Imagine that you were considering buying the whole company. How much would you be prepared to pay for the company and its $1 million of earnings? What price would you bid on that auction called the sharemarket? You might start to think of this in terms of the yield that you would get – just like the return that you would get from putting your money in the bank.

You might decide that if you could get 6% simply by putting your money in the bank, you would want a return of roughly double that to invest in a relatively risky company. You might therefore offer a price which will get you a 12.5% return.

That means that you would agree to pay $8m for the company.

$$\frac{\$1\text{m}}{\$8\text{m}} \times 100 = 12.5\%$$

This is logical – you have decided what return you require and offer a price that will get you that return. With a bit of luck the vendor will agree. However, if the vendor does not agree and wants more than $8m you may have to walk away from the deal. For example, if the vendor wants $10m, that would only give you a return of 10%, which does not meet your criterion of achieving twice the return that you could get at the bank.

Unfortunately, in business valuations the terminology is different, even though the principle is the same. Instead of thinking of the earnings yield, business valuers (and therefore sharemarket people) think about a price:earnings ratio, or put another way, how many times annual earnings (or profits) they are prepared to pay.

In the above example, if you wanted a yield of 12.5%, you would be paying eight times earnings. This is a P:E ratio of 8.

$$\text{P:E ratio} = \frac{\$8\text{m}}{\$1\text{m}} = 8$$

Note that arithmetically it is the inverse of the earnings yield. You will still get the same amount of profit/earnings for your money – only the means of expressing it has changed.

People in the sharemarket seldom talk about earnings yield – they nearly always talk about P:E ratios. They are assessing how many times annual earnings they will pay for a share. Note that they are looking at the total amount of profits that the company is earning after tax. It is not important that part of those profits is retained by the company while a part is paid out as dividends to shareholders.

If it is a 'good' company they will pay many times earnings (perhaps 20 times or more). This means a lower earnings yield. If it is a 'poor' company they will pay only a few times earnings (perhaps only five times) and therefore get a higher earnings yield.

What constitutes a good company (which therefore deserves a high P:E ratio) and what constitutes a poor company is mostly about whether or not the profits themselves are 'good'. Remember, the four things which make up good profits (see pages 101–102) are: sustainable profits, timing of profits, quality of profits and how likely they are to grow.

Unfortunately (and there are quite a lot of 'unfortunatelys' in this chapter!), few of us want to buy the whole company. Most of us only want to buy a *share* or a few thousand shares in the company. Therefore, we need to split the profit to find what profit is attributable to each individual share. This means dividing the profit by the number of shares in the company to give us an earnings per share (eps).

$$\text{earnings per share} = \frac{\text{profit}}{\text{shares on issue}}$$

If we find that the company has 5 million shares on issue and is making a profit of $1 million p.a., the earnings per share is:

$$\text{eps} = \frac{\$1\text{m}}{\$5\text{m}} = 20¢$$

Each share is earning 20c. Every share that you own is making a profit of 20c. This 20c per share may not be paid out to you in cash by way of dividends (some will be retained by the company), but that is what each share is earning.

Now, if we know what the earnings per share is and what the share price is we can calculate the P:E ratio:

$$\text{P:E ratio} = \frac{\text{share price}}{\text{shares on issue}}$$

Using our example above of a company with an eps of 20c, if the share price is 160c the P:E is:

$$P{:}E = \frac{160¢}{20¢} = 8$$

As an investor you might think that a P:E of 8 is quite low and that the quality of the company and its profits are such that it warrants a higher P:E ratio. You might think that it really warrants a P:E of, say, 12, because other comparable companies are trading at about 12. You can then calculate what you think would be a reasonable value for the share:

share value = fair P:E x eps

In this example, if you decided that the fair P:E was 12, the value of the share would be:

share value = 12 x .20¢ = 240¢

Clearly this share would rate as a 'buy' – it is currently trading at 160c but you think that it is worth 240c because it should have a higher P:E. Your next step is to buy at 160c and wait for the market to wake up and rate the share at a P:E of 12 as it should be.

This is basically what investors are looking for: shares which are trading on a P:E which is lower than is really warranted. It requires looking at other similar companies, especially those in the same industries. If other companies in that industry have higher P:E ratios, ultimately the market will see the worth of the company and push up its price until the P:E is appropriate (hopefully this happens the day after you have bought a good number of shares!).

The appropriate P:E might be:

good company	16–18
average company	12–14
poor company	8–10

Assessing what is an appropriate P:E for a company is perhaps the most difficult part of share investing and requires judgement. In the final analysis the market rates companies, deciding on the share price by saying what P:E ratio is appropriate and warranted. In effect the market rates the company according to its profits, their sustainability and likely growth. The market compares the quality of one company's profits with others in the same industry; it compares the prospects for one industry against other industries and rates whole economies against others. The market decides what is a reasonable P:E ratio (or average P:E ratio for an industry or economy) and sets prices accordingly.

> **Assessing what is an appropriate P:E for a company is perhaps the most difficult part of share investing . . .**

It is this that people are meaning when they say that a share is 'too expensive' or an industry is 'too highly rated'. In saying that, they do not mean that company's share price is too much in absolute terms – that one company's share price is 60c while another's is 460c. This is not what is meant as being too expensive. Instead, what is meant is that it is selling on a P:E that is too high – and of course the 60c company may have a higher P:E than the 460c one (depending on shares on issue and earnings).

As an investor you are looking for value by finding companies that are selling on P:Es which are lower than is warranted. You are looking for a company selling on a P:E of, say, 10, when a P:E of 15 is probably appropriate. You want to buy that company on a P:E of 10 and then wait for the market to wake up to how good it is, increasing its share price and so re-rating it to a P:E of 15. Conversely, you want to sell a company that is trading on a P:E of 30, when a P:E of 15 is warranted. Similarly, a market like the USA which had average P:Es of around 35 ten years ago was too expensive (and therefore collapsed) while New Zealand at the same time had average P:Es of 12 and therefore held up much better.

Unfortunately (again!), most wise investors do not assess a company and calculate the P:E on *last* year's profits. You are investing for the future, not for the past. Historic profit is irrelevant – it has been and gone. It is future or prospective profit that is important.

Therefore, you need to have some indication of what future profit might be. This can come from a number of sources:

- The company itself announces what it is expecting to earn.
- Sometimes the researchers at sharebrokers do company visits and make an estimate of profitability. These estimates are sometimes averaged and produced in tip sheets or other media as consensus.
- You might do your own research, looking at past performance and the company's stated plans and then making an educated guess.

Often, brokers and researchers will project profits (and therefore a company's P:E) forward for several years. Obviously, the further out the projections are made, the more difficult it is to make accurate predictions. However, you will often see charts like this:

	Y/E 2009 (actual)	Y/E 2010 (forecast)	Y/E 2011 (forecast)
eps	20¢	25¢	30¢
P:E (at 300¢)	15	12	10

As earnings rise, the P:E ratio will fall, assuming of course that the share price remains the same. In fact what is much more likely to happen is that the share price will rise as profitability rises, keeping the P:E around the 15 level, or even higher if the rate of growth of profits looks to be increasing faster.

DOUBLE WHAMMY

Growth in earnings leads to growth in share price. This happens even when the market continues to rate the company the same and so keeps its P:E ratio at about the same level. When this happens, the share price will rise in line with the growth in profitability.

However, what often happens is that as the market comes to recognise that this is a company which has good, sustainable and consistently growing profits, it will re-rate it. The market will push up the price and the shares will trade at a higher P:E.

Therefore, there are two factors pushing up the share price:

1. growth in earnings

2. higher P:E.

Imagine a company with an eps of 25c, trading at a P:E of 12. The share price is:

$$25¢ \times 12 = 300¢$$

Profits grow so that the earnings per share are now 30c. Assuming the P:E remains at 12, this would put the share price up to:

$$30¢ \times 12 = 360¢$$

However, at the same time the market decides that the company now warrants a higher P:E ratio, say 16. The price goes to:

$$30¢ \times 16 = 480¢$$

The market has pushed up the share price from 300c to 480c. In doing so it is accepting that a higher P:E is justified and, of course, that P:E is calculated on the higher earnings per share.

The stunning investment performance during the 1990s of Telecom was brought about by this double whammy. Telecom was floated at 200c. Its earnings per share were 14cps and at 200c the P:E was 14. The earnings per share rose to 47cps and the P:E, at around 20, gave it a share price of around 900c. Of course a fall in profitability will have the same effect but in reverse as Telecom investors have found more recently. The market will downgrade a company whose profits look vulnerable and apply a lower P:E in the assessment of value.

EARNINGS GROWTH

Earnings growth is what good investing is all about. If you can find businesses that keep on growing their profits, this extra profit will be reflected in the share price.

Note also that there is a compounding effect which comes

from earnings growth. Most companies hold on to most of their profits – they usually only pay a small amount out as dividends. The balance of the profits is retained in the business. These retained earnings are effectively profits that are being reinvested in the business. If the business is good, and especially if management is good, it will be able to use those reinvested profits to make even more profits.

> The market will downgrade a company whose profits look vulnerable and apply a lower P:E in the assessment of value.

NO DIVIDENDS, THANKS

Personally, I prefer companies that pay out only a little (or even nothing) by way of dividends. If the company is good I would prefer it retained its profits to make more money. If the company is not good, why am I investing in it? I do not really want to go to the trouble of banking a dividend and then reinvesting it in the company by buying more shares on the market. Better instead, for someone like me who is not particularly interested in income, for the company to keep its profits and keep expanding the business.

Some companies give their shareholders the option of taking shares in lieu of dividends. This means that instead of cash you get shares to the value of the dividend. I like this because it means my share of a company's profits is automatically being compounded. It is also good for companies that are growing strongly and needing all the capital they can get. If shareholders elect to take shares instead of cash dividends, the company keeps the profit that it would have paid out and can use it to fund growth.

HIGH P:E RATIOS

In some countries around the world, shares have traded on very high P:E ratios – it is not at all unusual for some companies to sell at 40 or 50 times earnings and some of the stellar performers at times to be on P:E ratios of 70 or higher. This has been because the performance of some companies and some markets has been so good that everyone wants to be in there. However, a company has to produce very good profits which grow at a high rate for these sorts of P:E ratios to be justified. This is seldom the case, and the more likely scenario is that the market falls. The average P:E ratio in the USA in 2000 was clearly too high, and share prices fell so that they were under 20.

PEG

Whether or not P:Es are too high really depends on the likely growth of earnings. PEGs are a way of measuring the price:earnings ratio compared to the company's growth in earnings per share. There is no problem with buying a share with a high P:E ratio provided that there is good enough growth in earnings to bring the P:E ratio down.

The PEG (price earnings and growth) is simple to calculate:

$$\text{PEG} = \frac{\text{P:E}}{\text{eps growth}}$$

For example, if a company was selling on a P:E of 15 and had earnings growth of 10% p.a., its PEG would be:

$$\text{PEG} = \frac{15}{10} = 1.5$$

It is generally thought that for a company to rate as a 'buy', it should have a PEG of 1 or less. That would mean it would have to have a P:E ratio the same as its annual growth rate. In the above example, to rate as a 'buy' either the share price would have to fall to bring its P:E ratio down to 10, or the growth in earnings would have to increase. Note that to calculate the earnings growth of a company, you should look back at least five years and take the average earnings per share growth over that time.

Many people would want to see a PEG significantly under 1 (perhaps 0.8) before they would rate a share a 'buy'. There is nothing magical about a PEG of 1. Looking at PEGs is simply a good way to see how highly the market is rating a share (by its

P:E) and seeing if its growth rate warrants that. While it is not spoken of much amongst New Zealand sharemarket investors yet, PEG is something that we are bound to hear more of in the future.

DIVIDEND YIELD

This is the second measure that is used to value a share. It measures the amount that you will receive in cash from the company by way of dividend over the course of a year, compared to the share price. It is a bit like the amount of interest that you get when you put your money in the bank: if you put $1000 in the bank and get $70 of interest each year, you are getting a 7% yield. Similarly with shares: if you buy a share for 100c and get 7c in dividends for the year, you have a dividend yield of 7%.

Most companies that are profitable pay out a part of their profits to their shareholders as dividends. Few companies pay all of their profit out as dividends, most preferring to hold some profit back in the company to fund growth. Similarly, few profitable companies pay out no dividends to their shareholders although there are some who make no (or very little) dividend payments each year.

Typically, a company will pay out between 30% and 50% of its profit, retaining the rest for growth. Usually a company will make two dividend payments each year, an interim dividend and a final dividend (there are a few companies which pay quarterly, usually because they are 'income' stocks and have large numbers of shareholders who want a regular income).

A typical company might pay two dividends:

interim dividend 15 May	4¢
final dividend 15 November	5¢
total payments	9¢

If this company's share price was 140c, the dividend yield would be:

$$\frac{\text{annual dividend}}{\text{share price}} \times 100 = \frac{9¢}{140¢} \times 100 = 6.4\%$$

This dividend is usually net, or tax-paid. The company has already paid tax on its profits and therefore pays the profits to the shareholders with imputation credits so that they pay no more tax (depending on their tax rate – see Chapter Four).

The dividend yield is not the best indicator of company value because it can vary so much, depending upon each company's dividend policy. For example, two companies each paying out 9c a year in dividends to their shareholders might have quite different share valuations because one is paying out 35% of its profit while the other is paying out 75%. The one which is paying out 35% of its profit would be more valuable because the remaining 65% of the profit is held in the company and used either to buy new assets or reduce debt. Either way, shareholder value is enhanced because it is the shareholders who own the profits that are held in the company, regardless of what they are used for.

Nevertheless, although dividend yield is not the purest measure of the company's performance, many investors buy or sell on the basis of it. This is because it does give a broad measure of investment value but, more importantly, there are many investors who depend on income from dividends to live on. These people often look for high-yielding shares. Such shares do not usually provide such good growth in share price because they are not retaining much profit for growth. However, although that may be generally true, there are many instances of high dividend shares being 'discovered' by the market and being bought up so that the price rises strongly.

> Although dividend yield is not the purest measure of the company's performance, many investors buy or sell on the basis of it.

Dividend yield works especially well as a broad measure of value when compared to other investments such as bank deposits or bonds. These are the alternative income investments for many people. If dividend yields (either for a target company or for the market as a whole) are substantially below bonds or bank deposits it may be that the market is getting too high. However, if dividend yields are above these alternative investments, it is likely that before too long investors will start putting more money into shares and so push up prices. Some companies (especially utilities and property companies) respond very quickly to changes in interest rates: a rise in interest rates pulls the share price down; a fall in interest rates pushes it up. This is because many investors in these industries are looking for a good dividend to live on and compare their dividend returns with what they might get in the bank. Some of these companies pay out nearly all of their profits as dividends, making them ideal income stocks.

Dividend yield is frequently used to try to establish whether the market overall represents good value. As such, it can be used to help with timing and in deciding whether a particular time is a good time to buy.

Australian author Austin Donnelly, in his book *Sensible Share Investing – Better Results Through Careful Timing*, uses the experience and records that he has accumulated over 35 years to come up with a system that indicates with some reliability whether or not it is a good time to buy. Donnelly looks at dividend yields and puts them in five zones:

Zone 1	2.2% to 3.69%
Zone 2	3.7% to 4.09%
Zone 3	4.1% to 4.59%
Zone 4	4.6% to 4.49%
Zone 5	5.5% and above

What Donnelly found was that if you bought when dividend yields were high you would get a far better future return with far less chance of downside risk than if you bought when they were low. For example, if you bought shares when dividends were in Zone 5 you would get a total return on average of 14.9%; if you bought shares in Zone 1, your average return would be 0.6%.

This is hardly surprising, of course. High dividend yields reflect low share price. Buying at a time of high dividend yield not only gets you a better dividend but also means that you are buying into a depressed market which will recover. Obvious though all of this may seem, Donnelly's system seems an easy, practical way to judge whether it is a favourable or unfavourable time to buy. I recommend Donnelly's book to anyone interested in investing in shares.

NET TANGIBLE ASSET BACKING

This is the third major indicator of value. It looks at the net tangible assets (nta) that a company has after deducting liabilities. As such it gives an indication of the amount that each shareholder would receive if the company stopped trading, sold off all its assets, repaid all debts and gave the balance back to shareholders. It is usually the least important measure of a share's value.

Note the nta only looks at tangible assets like plant and equipment, stock, property, etc. It takes no account of the intangibles like any goodwill value, brands, trademarks, etc. Looking at nta gives a fallback position, a level of safety – if things turn bad for a company which has a high nta, the shareholder should be able to get most of the investment back. For example, my gold pen with its (unreal) $100,000 income is worth $1m. However, the nta is only $300 so if the income stopped for any reason the owner of it would only be able to recover $300 by selling the pen and so have to write off as a loss nearly all of the $1m paid for it.

Nta is calculated by dividing the net assets of the company by the number of shares on issue. Take Fisher & Paykel Healthcare (FPH) as an example:

total assets	$472m
total liabilities	($199m)
net assets	$273m

These figures come from the company's balance sheet. FPH has 509 million shares on issue.

$$\text{net assets per share} = \frac{\$273\text{m}}{509\text{m}} = 54 \text{ cents per share}$$

If FPH was broken up, shareholders would receive 54c for each share that they hold.

However, FPH's share price is around 330c. Why would people pay 330c for only 54 cents' worth of assets? The answer to that is that FPH is earning good profits – it is using its assets efficiently. The difference between the 330c that people are prepared to pay for a FPH share and the 54c of tangible assets is goodwill and the value of its brand. Investors know that FPH is a company that has a good track record of profitability, has excellent products that would be hard for a competitor to duplicate, and has a vision and plans for expansion. Investors therefore value FPH on the basis of its profits (by way of its P:E ratio) and largely ignore its nta.

This is in fact very common for a lot of companies. To an extent, most investors do not care about the nature of the assets or their value – what they care most about is the profits that the company's directors can generate from those assets. My seminar audiences will pay only a little for my gold pen as a tangible asset but will pay much more if it is an ongoing business with good profits. They don't care about the pen's replacement or break-up value. They only care about the profits and their quality.

Nta is usually only important if the company is performing poorly or if it is in an industry which is easy to enter. If it is an easy-entry industry, a competitor could come along, duplicate the assets and start trading in competition. Profitable companies in areas where competitors would find it hard to enter the market (e.g. FPH) tend to have share prices well in excess of nta. For these companies, nta is almost an irrelevance.

However, there are situations where nta is an important measure of value. Forestry companies are usually valued by their nta (although they often trade below their net assets). Property investment companies are also usually valued by their nta. In New Zealand, some property companies have a share price below their nta (Property For Industry is an exception here).

Investors will take a lot of notice of nta if the company is struggling and making losses. There is a degree of safety in knowing that, theoretically at least, the company could be broken up and the shareholders get their money back. This is a bit theoretical because in a liquidation situation the assets will not fetch the value that they are on the company's books at. Sometimes if a company is doing especially poorly it will trade at a discount to nta.

> There is a degree of safety in knowing that, theoretically at least, the company could be broken up and the shareholders get their money back.

Although there are these exceptions, nta is generally not the most important item in your search for value. True, it is something that you should always look at before buying shares. However, you should not be put off buying into a company which has a low nta relative to its share price as long as it is making good profits and has a reasonably low P:E ratio and/or high dividend yield.

The most important thing in buying companies (or shares in companies) is always going to be the profits that they make. That is the entire point of buying into a company – profits! The shares in the company must be valued by those profits – that is, by way of the P:E ratio.

You cannot hope to beat the market without being able to identify value. You cannot hope to know value without understanding P:E ratios, dividend yields and nta ratios. There are other indicators of value but these are the bare minimum. Whether you do the research yourself or simply read tip sheets, brokers' reports or the business pages of the local newspaper, you must understand these three things. Only when you do can you be sure that you are buying value.

A TIME TO SELL

Much of this chapter is about choosing shares which are good to *buy*. Picking shares which are good to *sell* is simply the reverse. Shares which are good to sell are ones that no longer represent good value: the business that the company owns and operates is no longer performing. This may also apply to whole markets: in 2008 I became worried about the poor value represented by markets and sold out of shares almost completely (a good move as it transpired).

> **If you are a long-term investor, you are not going to sell very much.**

If you are a long-term investor, you are not going to sell very much. You will have bought into good businesses which will perform over the long term and simply ride out the falls in value knowing that there will be even greater rises coming soon. As a long-term investor you know that your greatest virtues are patience and good nerves. It is only at times when values are a long way out of line that you should sell down.

Your trading portfolio is of course quite different. However, your concern with your investments is not about the noise of the markets or what the flighty reef fish are saying and doing. The market is secondary to the performance of your businesses.

Nevertheless, there are times to sell. You cannot simply forget your shares once you have bought them – the activity of the companies and the underlying trends to the business need constant scrutiny and management.

RATE YOUR SHARES

One of the things you may do quite regularly is adjust your portfolio. This may mean selling something and putting more money into something that you already own. A useful tip to manage this is to give each of your holdings a performance rating – each share is given a priority in terms of how well you think the business is doing. This would mean that if you owned six shares you would rate them 1 to 6 (1 being the best, 6 being the worst). The ones rated 5 or 6 would be constantly watched and if more money was required for one of your top-rating companies (or if you simply need to cash up) it would be one of these two that would be sold.

Clearly you should have more money in your shares that are rated 1 or 2 than those that are rated 5 or 6. Of course, if you took this to its logical conclusion you would end up with just one company. I am not advocating that – most investors should hold at least four companies and possibly as many as ten. The key to rating shares is to avoid emotion. You need to assess what you have in terms of likely future performance. This has nothing to do with how well they have done in the past or any sort of emotional attachment that you might have to them.

> You need to assess what you have in terms of likely future performance.

If shares have performed well in the past, it is very easy to carry on holding them even though you know that the business is not performing as well as it was and there are good reasons for its likely future underperformance. Holding on, hoping against hope that past glory will be restored is explicable by behavioural psychology. The previous good performance rewarded your behaviour in owning the shares, and so like Pavlov's dog you continue the behaviour even though the reward is no longer really there. Pavlov's dog salivated when the dinner bell was sounded even though food was no longer provided. Habits die hard and you can easily let the habit of owning a share continue even when deep down you know it's a habit that you should kick. Your head must rule – get rid of bad habits.

WHEN TO SELL AND WHEN NOT TO SELL

With all of this in mind, it is useful to look at what should prompt you to sell and what should not.

Do not sell when:

- Your share has been re-rated to a high P:E ratio and the share price has gone up with it. Many people do not let their profits run – the share price (and P:E) go up and so they take their profits. Unless the P:E has gone to ridiculous levels, the re-rating of your company is actually a good thing. If the P:E has gone from 10 to 20, that means that every bit of extra profit will be multiplied by 20 to get the share price instead of 10. A high P:E is usually the market's recognition that the business is performing well. Why do you want to sell a good business?

- There is market weakness. The sharemarket is cyclical and largely driven by people who think short term. That is no reason for you to bail out of good businesses – it is probably instead a time to buy some more of them.

- There is a poor profit result. This happens quite frequently to even the best businesses. One bad profit does not make a bad business.

- Loss of a senior manager. This is one of those things that often causes investor flight when it is not justified. No one is irreplaceable – ask yourself if this resigning executive was really that good and if no one else could do the job.

- There are cyclical economic events. Things like a high or low dollar, high interest rates, recessions and high inflation may make it more difficult to run a business but these things come and go. A good business should be able to trade well even when there is some inflation and, although higher interest rates will cut into profits, it probably will not be by that much. In any event, a high dollar is followed by a low dollar, a recession is followed by expansion, etc – these economic events are cyclical.

Sell when:

- There is a declining business trend. Serious business problems usually happen slowly over a long period of time – seldom does a good business turn into a bad one overnight. Instead there is a gradual loss of market share, perhaps a series of poor management decisions which become apparent over time. You won't recognise these trends immediately as they happen, but when you do see them, it's time to sell.
- There is poor brand management. For some businesses, the brand is one of their most valuable assets. I have always thought that if The Warehouse ever started to put plush carpet on the floors of their shops, changed the bright red barn to a building painted light brown and started emphasising quality instead of price in their advertising, these things would be a sure sign that the company had forgotten what it was and had lost its way. That would be a time to sell.
- There is major market dislocation. By this I am thinking of the sharemarket crash of 1987 or the dot-com crash of 2001 or the Great Recession of 2008–2009. On the day before the 1987 crash, the day of it and within a couple of days afterwards, I sold everything that I had. I recognised that the world had changed – the times that had been so kind for nearly a decade were gone. When such a thing happens, be decisive and dump everything, even though prices are comparatively low.
- Management of your company becomes overly concerned about the share price. I think the role of managers is to run the business to make a profit. I get concerned when I see directors and company managers trying to put their results in the best light possible and seeming to run a PR campaign. If the managers simply get on with making good profits,

> I am not fond of managers being given large numbers of share options as 'incentives'. . .

the share price will look after itself. Good companies do not need glitzy PR to their shareholders and prospective shareholders – they should put their efforts into communicating with the customers. This is one of the reasons that I am not fond of managers being given large numbers of share options as 'incentives' – if they are good professionals and are well paid, they shouldn't need any more rewards.

- Companies have ridiculous valuations. There are times when companies do have ridiculous valuations: P:Es of 70 or more without the profit growth to justify it. Remember that your P:E to growth ratio (PEG) should be less than one. That figure is not carved in stone but a PEG of, say, 2, would be a strong sell indicator unless there was something special.

The decision whether to be a bull and buy or hold on, or to be a bear and sell, largely comes down to focusing single-mindedly on what it is that you are doing – buying and selling businesses. Ask yourself: do you really want to own this business? The ultimate judgement probably comes from the answer to this question. Imagine that you were given a substantial amount of money to invest. Would you buy more of the companies that you already hold? If the answer is no to any one of them, you would then want to ask yourself why you are owning it. If you do not have enough confidence to put more money into a company, you have something which probably rates a 'sell'.

WAY THREE

Limit your trading

Smart investors make most of their money by buying into good businesses and holding on to them. But smart investors like to play as well. Just because you are a long-term investor and make most of your money that way, there is no reason why you cannot be opportunistic and do some trading. Today, with screen trading, market access via the Internet and lower brokerage fees, this is far more possible than it ever was.

Smart investors do not confuse their 'play' money with their serious investment funds. Instead they dedicate a certain amount or proportion of their funds to both activities. In effect, they limit their trading to a pre-set and planned amount of money. Trading is riskier than investment and only a limited amount of money should be used for it. Generally, 10–20% of total funds should be set aside to try and take advantage of some of the special situations and opportunities which arise.

There are some people who believe that you should buy into the market via a good spread of shares or even through an index tracker and simply hold that forever. It is a good enough strategy for those who are content with being ordinary, who don't want to beat the market. However, nearly everyone that I know who is in shares at some point or other looks for something special.

> **Nearly everyone takes a short-term position on a share, hoping for a quick profit. That is a part of the game.**

Nearly everyone takes a short-term position on a share, hoping for a quick profit. That is a part of the game. Just don't let it be a big part of the game.

SENSIBLE TRADING

Sensible trading will put you ahead of the market. The profits that you make are over and above those from your long-term investment holdings. The words 'sensible trading' will seem to be contradictory to some people – there is no such thing as trading which is sensible, according to some! A lot of people think that it is impossible to profit from trading over the long haul.

In fact, I think that you can. To me, sensible trading is using a part of your available funds to take relatively short-term positions in companies. This is not your core investment portfolio – that is in quality companies which are being held long term. It is the last 10–20% of your sharemarket funds that you use to have fun and make money with, to try to get ahead of the market average. The key to successful trading is to limit it to a pre-set amount of money and then stick to that.

For example, you might have $100,000 allocated for sharemarket investment. The bulk of that money will be in a good solid portfolio of high-value performers. It might look like this:

NZ 10	$ 30,000
NZX Mid-Cap	$ 10,000
GPG	$ 10,000
Ryman Healthcare	$ 10,000
Ebos Group	$ 10,000
Property for Industry	$ 5000
Contact Energy	$ 5000
Infratil	$ 5000
	$ 85,000

The balance can be used for short-term trades, for special situations and for new floats as they arise.

It is not true (as some people say) that you cannot be successful with this money. It is true that you will not profit from every opportunity that comes along – you will miss some. It is also true that you will occasionally make mistakes that will be costly. However, you should be able to do some highly profitable trades with this money and get yourself an above-average return from your total share capital.

To make these trades profitable, you need a system, or some rules – and the discipline to stick to it. This trading cannot be done on a whim. It must be clearly thought out. You should also beware the temptation to put more than the money that you have allocated into the market. It is easy to start dipping into other funds that you have or to cash up some shares that you hold in your long-term portfolio. I have known people to believe in themselves and their trading success so much that they are prepared to load up their credit cards or use their tax money for speculative trades. Sooner or later you are bound to make a bad call – losing money is one thing; trouble with Visa is quite another.

COVER THE DOWNSIDE

The first rule of trading, indeed of any investing, is attitudinal: it is to cover the downside. This means a safety-first approach. Losses can quickly wreck what has been a good trading performance. Trading is a risky activity – you will always have some losses. The secret is to make sure that they are neither too frequent nor too big. Even one big loss can bring you back to your starting point or underneath it. The old saying 'if in doubt stay out' is very true. You are better to pass up an opportunity if you are not completely confident – there will be more opportunities coming along soon enough.

Losses can quickly wreck what has been a good trading performance.

The Achilles heel of many traders is often overconfidence. Initial success is rewarded, leading to feelings of invulnerability; these feelings override what should be primary: *thinking*. You need to tell yourself all of the time that you can lose, that there are risks. If you are buying, there is someone else who is selling and this seller has reasons. Before ever going into a trade you should know all of the pros and cons of the trade and be very sure that the pros substantially outweigh the cons. As a simple exercise, write down the reasons why people might be selling. When you have identified them, jot down your reasons for buying. If your reasons are not more weighty than the sellers' reasons by a long way, forget the trade: put safety first.

Investing does not have quite the same problems. Investors know that the seller may be quitting their shares for any reason: taking profits from a trade, frightened by a rise or fall in the exchange rate, cashing up to take a holiday, etc. None of these things impact on the investor's decision because he or she is focused on buying into a business and what the share price does shortly after this is of only minor concern. The investor is concerned about the business's performance and should be confident in the analysis of that. Investors know that the value of the business will be reflected in the share price eventually. The investor is looking for long-term profits and is using short-term feelers to buy good businesses at fair prices.

Traders, however, have to get their judgement right from the very beginning. The shares that they are trading may not be good businesses and they certainly do not want to hang on to them for long. Time is not on their side, nor necessarily is the quality of what they are holding: nearly every trader at times buys into shares that he or she knows are rubbish, hoping that the market will recognise it for what it is only *after* he or she has sold on.

> Traders have to get their judgement right from the very beginning.

SET LIMITS

When investing, I never care too much about a few cents on the price. I don't think that it makes much difference in the long run whether I buy GPG at 80c or 84c – the important thing is that the analysis is right and that I own the shares. If I think the shares are really worth, say, 200c, they are a good investment whether they were bought at 80c or 84c.

This is not so with trading, where a few cents does make a difference. Therefore set limits for each of your trades – if you cannot buy the share within those limits, be prepared to walk away. There will always be other opportunities.

The limits that you set may be on a number of things:

- The price that you are prepared to pay for the shares.
- The price at which you will sell. For most trading this should represent a 10–20% profit (it hardly seems worth it if there is not 10–20% in the deal). However, do not be too firm on this target, especially if what you have bought is doing well. If you have profits running strongly, let them keep running, do not sell just because the shares have reached your target and given you a 20% profit.

> To protect the downside set a limit beneath what you have paid and resolve to sell if the shares fall to that value.

- The price at which you will sell if the shares are not performing: a stop-loss limit. You need to protect the downside and the best way of doing that is to set a limit beneath what you have paid (say 10% below) and resolve to sell if the shares fall to that value. This will cut your losses before they become too serious.
- The time at which you are going to sell. This is especially important with stagging shares. Think about whether you are going to sell on the day of listing or try to pick your time within a few days of listing. My preference is to sell on the day of listing, especially if the issue has closed oversubscribed. If you hold on longer, you are really trying to second-guess the market, something which you may be able to do but at which you may fail.

- The amount of money that goes into any one trade should have a limit. This may be in dollar terms (e.g. no more than $10,000 into any short-term deal) or as a percentage (e.g. no more than 50% of trading funds to go into any one trade).

These limits are designed to take some of the risk out of your trading. None of them are binding or unable to be broken, but if you set yourself some rules you should think twice before you break them. As such they act as a check, forcing you to hesitate before you put all your money on one deal or hold on to some shares even though they are falling in value. Setting limits and rules imposes a discipline on you so that you are making decisions with your head at a quiet time, rather than making snap decisions on the basis of how you feel.

WHAT IS TRADING?

Trading is usually taking advantage of short-term market inefficiencies. The market is not totally efficient – there are times when the value of a share might not reflect all of the known information. In any event, some market players are better informed than others. Over time, the market gives the true value of a share but this is not always true in the short term. Because the market is not entirely rational (it is often driven by the emotions of fear and greed) there are gaps between price and value.

There are three main areas that give opportunities for short-term trading profits:

1. Stagging new listings.

2. Timing the market.

3. Special situations.

STAGGING NEW LISTINGS

Stagging new shares has already been mentioned in this book. It deserves prominence because it is such an important way to profit from shares. It is an activity that should be enthusiastically embraced by anyone with an interest in the sharemarket; it requires little skill and consistently produces good profits. It is a very easy way to ensure that you beat the market.

Stagging shares is taking up an allocation of shares in companies that are offered to the public and selling them as soon as they list on the sharemarket. Shares are offered to the public either directly through advertising or through sharebrokers. This floating is called an Initial Public Offering (IPO). Once the shares have been allocated, the company lists on the sharemarket and the shares you have can be sold.

As a matter of principle, you should take up any shares that you can get in an IPO, almost regardless of the price. Over the last few years, most companies that have sold shares to the public and then listed have come onto the market above the issue price.

Sometimes the company will do well after it has been floated on the sharemarket (e.g. Auckland International Airport, Pumpkin Patch) – sometimes it will do badly (e.g. Restaurant Brands, Kathmandu, Feltex). However, whatever has happened subsequently, most companies have débuted onto the market at a price above what they were sold to the public at.

You should take advantage of this: make a policy of buying every share which is offered to the public and which is going to be listed. If you sell on the day of listing or shortly thereafter you are almost certain to make money. You may lose on the odd one but you will win on far more. The only exception to this rule would be property company shares, forestry shares and some of the small companies which list on NZAX (the alternative market for smaller developing companies) which have not been as consistent for the stags. Exercise some discretion with these.

If you sell on the day of listing or shortly thereafter you are almost certain to make money.

Whether you hold any IPOs that you get is also a matter of discretion. There are some shares which should not be stagged – e.g. Pumpkin Patch, good quality shares which fit into the long-term hold part of your portfolio well. You may buy these during the IPO, even buying more after they list. Set your strategy and plan according to the analysis that you have done.

This is one of the reasons that you want a good relationship with your sharebroker. Some IPOs are sold direct, like Contact Energy. Others, however, are sold through brokers who get a firm allocation of shares which they can sell on to their clients. Many IPOs are a scramble to get enough shares. A good relationship with a broker may mean that you will consistently get some of the allocation. This may be even more important in the next year or two, as the NZX works hard to increase the number of companies listing on the market. Stags may enjoy their best period for a long time.

TIMING THE MARKET

This is far more difficult than stagging and in the long run not as profitable. It is less profitable simply because you are bound to get your timing wrong and make losses far more often than when stagging shares. Trying to time the market means playing the short-term wrinkles, rather than identifying long-term business trends.

Timing the market means buying a share at a time when the price is low and selling it on a rise. It is an awful lot easier to write this than it is to do! Timing the market is difficult because the market for any share is always in balance – buyers and sellers are in roughly equal numbers at a particular price level. As soon as the number of buyers and sellers moves out of equal numbers, the price will move very quickly to find equilibrium.

> **Because timing the market is so difficult, you should not expect great profits from it.**

Because timing the market is so difficult, you should not expect great profits from it. Indeed, you should set profit targets that are quite modest, forgoing some profit by not holding out for those last few cents.

LET THE OTHER GUY MAKE A PROFIT

I think that this is an important rule for all trading, but especially so if you are trying to profit from timing the market. It means not being too greedy. It means not even attempting to buy right at the bottom nor sell right at the top. The time to buy is after the shares have started to move up: the time to sell is while the shares are still rising, before they hit their peak.

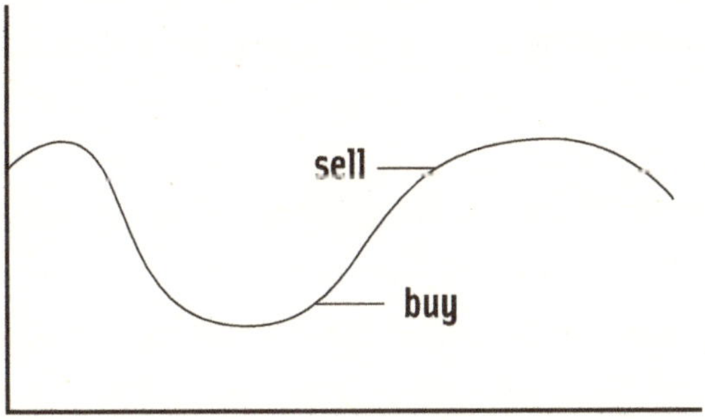

This means that your profit is significantly reduced. However, deliberately not trying to wring the last dollar of profit out of a trade reduces risk. I think it is better to give up some projected profit if you can give up some risk with it.

There is no foolproof way to time the market. People have tried all sorts of techniques and although some might be useful to an extent, there is no such thing as a surefire system.

CHARTING

Technical analysis (or charting) in all of its various forms is promoted by some as helping to time buy and sell decisions (see Way Six). I have some scepticism regarding its overall use and do not use it myself. Even the most wild-eyed charting enthusiast does not believe that technical analysis always gives the perfect answer. My view on charting is that for those who adopt it, study it and carry it through properly, it is probably of some help in timing the market. However, this needs to be done properly and consistently – you can't dabble with charting. Not many people will want to do enough trading to make the time, effort and expense (for those buying into computer programs) worthwhile.

MOVING AVERAGE

If there was one piece of technical analysis that I was going to use it would be the moving average. This involves having a line graph of a company's share price along with a line graph of the moving average. The moving average is a graph of the average that the share price has been at over a period of 30, 60, 100 or 200 days (you choose what time period you want). The moving average takes the closing price of the share for each of the days and averages it. It moves because each new closing price that comes into the calculation means that the last one drops off.

As such it gives you the average historical price for the period in which you are interested. You can compare this on your graph with the current price. What you are looking for is trends, specifically when the share price line breaks through (either above or below) the moving average line. When the share price line breaks above the moving average line, you have an indication to buy – and vice versa.

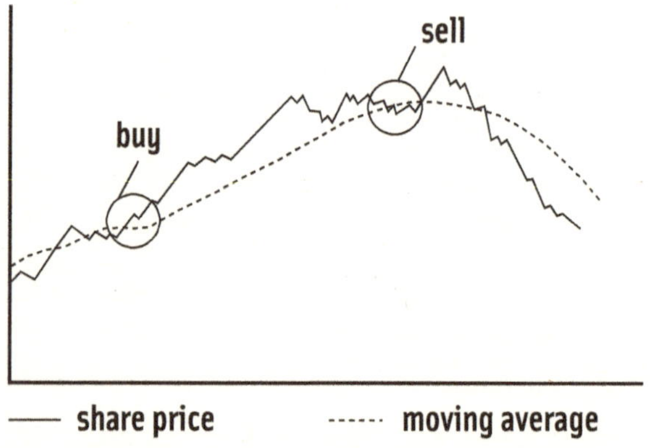

The time period that you use for the moving average depends on whether you are trading short- or long-term. A 30-day moving average would be used by short-term traders, 200 days by longer-term traders. Fortunately you do not have to do the moving average or graphing yourself. Charts are available on the Internet which are already done for you: many websites now will give you at least the basic charts.

There is a logic to using the moving average as an indicator as to whether it is a time to buy or sell – it is showing the break in a trend. The trouble is that quite often you get false starts – the share price line cuts the average line but then breaks back again. For that reason, most people using it wait until there is a clear break of the line before acting. This may cut your profits a bit but does reduce risk.

CHANNELLING

People usually profit through timing because shares will trade within a range. The shares trade in a range, or a channel, which may be around 10–20%. A good trader will try to buy at the bottom of the range and sell towards the top.

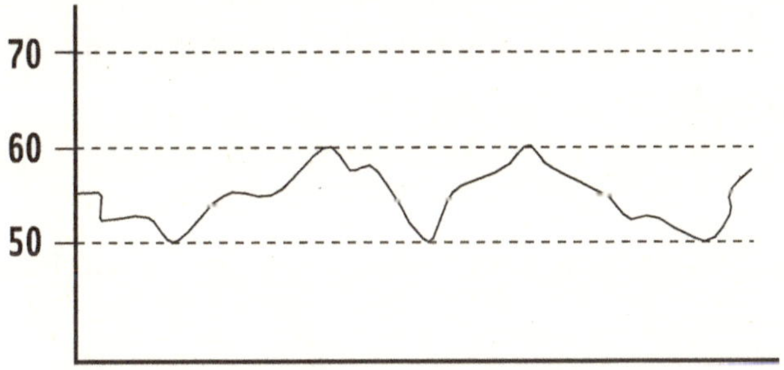

This graph shows a (fictitious) share price trading over time within a range of 50c and 60c. If you watch shares closely, you might be surprised how many shares do this and how long they do it for (often months and even years). In fact there is a good rationale for what is happening: each time the shares come down to near 50c, the market is saying that this is a cheap price and so buyers come in. As the price approaches 60c, the market thinks that these shares are getting overvalued and so people start to sell.

Certain shares can bounce around within a channel like this giving opportunities for buying and selling several times over. Once you recognise the pattern you can start to profit reasonably safely. You may want to graph the movement of the shares (a

> **Certain shares can bounce around within a channel giving opportunities for buying and selling several times over.**

simple form of charting) to help recognise the price levels where there is support and resistance, although many people do not bother as they get a feel for what is happening without drawing a picture.

Note that with the above example, the time to buy is not at 50c, nor the time to sell at 60c. Instead you would probably play for safety, buying at 52c and selling at around 58c. This is not the maximum profit but nevertheless is acceptable at around 13%. If you could do that a few times a year you would be making good money. Never try to pick the absolute bottom and buy while the share is still falling. Instead, let it fall, develop a base and then start to move up before you buy. Conversely, selling should be done before the share reaches its peak, while it is still rising. Only one person buys at the bottom; only one person sells at the top – the chances are not good that it will be you.

DOWNSIDE

The risk in channelling is of course that something happens and the shares stop trading in that range. Perhaps you have bought at 52c and the share suddenly drops below its previous support level of 50c. The important thing here is to act quickly, cut your losses and sell. Do not hold on, waiting and hoping that the previous share price behaviour will return – it probably won't. This is one of the reasons why it is usually better to do this kind of trading with quality shares: they are less likely to break that support level and collapse because there will always be investors looking to pick up shares at lower levels – nevertheless, if the shares do break out on the downside, cut and run.

It is probably best to try and trade like this with only one or two shares. I think you are better to watch and follow the price behaviour of just one share, and do that well, than try to track and trade a whole bunch. Trading by timing the market is the most difficult way to make money. Anything can go wrong – and often will. Concentrate on just one or two shares and try to make a little money out of them. Be very cautious and never be greedy – no one ever went broke making a profit.

> **Never be greedy – no one ever went broke making a profit.**

RIGHTS TRADING

Another good time to buy is after a cash issue has been announced and the rights to take up new shares are being traded on the market. Not all shareholders have the cash to take up the new shares that they are offered and so sell some or all of their rights. This sees a flood of shares come onto the market, depressing the price. The very fact that the company is asking its shareholders for more cash can be somewhat negative for a start, but the large number of shares that are for sale during rights trading pushes down the share price even further. Rights trading represents a very good time to buy – after the rights trading period is finished and the company has banked the cash from its shareholders, the price usually bounces back quite strongly (a good time to sell, if you are trading).

SPECIAL SITUATIONS

This third category of trading is potentially the most profitable for those who keep up with the play and are well informed. It is a broad category covering just about everything imaginable that can happen to a company.

Special situations are good for opportunists, for those who are ready and able to move quickly. They may also be for people with patience: there are often situations where it seems obvious that a share should rise in value but instead it will just sit, languishing for weeks or even months. This, no doubt, is because there is a big seller (perhaps an institution or an overseas investor) that is cashing up for its own reasons – nothing much will happen to the share price until they are all sold.

A good example of this was farm services company Wrightsons, which had had its problems: farmers had been struggling, Wrightsons tried to restructure (not very successfully) and to the surprise of many sold its finance company. All of this added up to a loss of over $9m in 1999.

The shares traded mostly at around 40 cents. However, they had a net tangible asset backing of over 70 cents and the rural sector was starting to pick up strongly. Then in late 1999 Sir Ron Brierley's GPG bought about 20% of the company – something looked like it might be happening. The shares seemed an obvious buy in January 2000 at 40 cents. However, for six months (it seemed like six years) nothing happened. It wasn't until June 2000 that the share price really started to move, going to over 65 cents.

That seemed like a long wait, but it pays to keep things in perspective. The share price going from 40c to 65c represents a profit of over 50% – you shouldn't ever expect that sort of profit overnight. It was surprising to me that the shares did not move sooner but good profits were there eventually in any event.

In many ways Wrightsons is a good example of a trade. They might not be a company that you would want to own as a long-term investment but their financial fundamentals (in terms of net asset backing), the recovery of their industry and the possibility of a corporate play (GPG) all pointed to a good short-term trade. Perhaps best of all there seemed limited downside – the shares were near their historic lows, farming was recovering (it didn't seem to be able to get much worse) and if GPG thought the shares were worth 40c, who are we to argue?

TAKEOVER

Takeovers of companies, or even the prospect of a takeover, represent the best opportunities for short-term profits. When one company wants to take over another it almost always has to pay a price that is higher than the price that prevails on the market. That provides a windfall for shareholders.

The secret to profiting from takeovers is to identify in advance companies that are likely to be taken over. This might sound difficult but is often in fact not terribly hard at all. Sometimes a prospective takeover is widely covered in the media, long before anything is announced. While this media coverage will get the share price moving, it will often not move as far as it should, leaving plenty of profit for new shareholders.

Identifying takeover targets does not require inside information nor top analytical skills – it is not that hard. Insider trading would of course be helpful but it is both illegal and immoral. Sometimes a takeover announcement comes as a surprise.

> Takeovers of companies . . . represent the best opportunities for short-term profits.

TAKEOVER TARGETS

Companies that are likely to be taken over by another are usually ones which are not profitable enough given the scope and size of their assets. There are plenty of exceptions to this, but generally a company will get picked off when its profits are too low and its share price is therefore only a little above net asset backing (or sometimes not above it at all). In essence, the target company is not using its assets efficiently, the market values its shares at a low level and so a predator comes in to buy those shares because it believes it can use the takeover target's assets more efficiently.

Your job is to identify companies that may get taken over, buy their shares and then wait. Identifying them is largely about keeping yourself informed – there is no great need to be clever because many potential takeovers are foreshadowed months, even years, in advance. You could trade well by simply taking up shares in takeover targets that have been discussed widely in the media. Certainly you may not be in on the ground floor and therefore not make the maximum amount of profit, but you will do well enough nevertheless.

To do better requires more detailed analysis. Any substantial premium over net asset backing will tend to put other companies off attempting takeovers. Note that you may have to wait for months or even years for the takeover to happen – but if you have picked the right company, it is only a matter of time before someone comes along to buy cheap assets.

PREDATORS

Other takeover prospects come about if a particular company has a key business that another might want.

The companies involved in trying to buy out the target may have one of two motivations:

1. They may want to asset strip the company. This means that the predator buys the target company at under net asset backing and then unlocks value by selling off the assets. There is a profit for the predator because it will sell off the assets at more than what it paid for them and it will perhaps keep one or two well-performing divisions going. Asset stripping was once very common (Brierley Investments raided companies in this way for a couple of decades) but no longer happens as often. Companies like GPG will buy into struggling businesses which are rich in assets, but they generally now work to rationalise the business (or even the whole industry) rather than simply strip out assets.

2. They may want to integrate the assets into their own. Very often one company sees that there will be savings in scale by adding another business, or it is looking for another part of the supply chain in its own industry. For example, a tourism coach line may want to add a chain of booking offices, or a bank buys an insurance company to add to its business.

HOSTILE TAKEOVERS

Not all takeover bids are welcomed by the takeover target. The bid is usually unwelcome because the directors believe that the price is not good enough. Such hostile takeovers can result in major fights and ultimately not go ahead. Sometimes the directors of the target company will look around for another predator to make an offer which is higher than the first takeover and in doing so try to create a bidding war for the benefit of the target.

Some takeovers are off-market. This means that the predator writes to shareholders directly, offering to buy their shares. You do not have to accept this offer, although if the predator gets acceptance of the offer from over 90% of the shareholders it can move to compulsorily acquire the remaining 10% of the shares. The compulsory acquisition is unlikely to be less than the offer made to shareholders and will sometimes be significantly more – it may be in your interest to hold out for as long as possible.

The best takeover opportunities often come when there is already a major shareholder (sometimes called a cornerstone shareholder) – one which may want to buy out the remaining shares to take full ownership. There are many examples of this, Stephen Tindall's attempt to buy out the other shareholders in The Warehouse being one. This resulted in a significant boost to the share price, even though it was not ultimately successful.

All trading, but especially profiting from special situations, is opportunistic. To do it successfully requires being well informed – you have to read everything and watch the markets. It also requires knowing the rules of the game and following them.

RULES OF THE GAME

1. **If in doubt stay out.** There is always at least some doubt when buying shares to trade – after all, for you to be able to buy, someone must be selling and have some reasons for doing so. Be decisive! In share trading there is no such thing as 'hold'. On any particular share you are either a bull or a bear, you are either in or are out.

2. **Trade in quality shares.** You will not always be able to do this but there is a margin of safety when you can. Quality shares are unlikely to suddenly slump in value whereas penny dreadfuls

can see the small bit of value that they did have vanish overnight.

3. **Trade in thick markets.** A thick market is one where there is always a lot of buying and selling going on, making it much easier for you to get in and get out again.

   Thin markets, shares which are only seldom traded and only in small volumes, are dangerous as just one buyer or seller can push the price strongly in a particular direction. This causes anomalies that may be to your disadvantage.

4. **Start small.** Don't commit too much of your money to trading generally, or to one share in particular, early on in your share trading career. Successful trading may take years, even decades – and even then you will still make mistakes. Don't let one big mistake take you out of the game before you have properly got started.

> A few small profits are just as good as one big one.

5. **Take your profits.** No one ever went broke by making a profit. A few small profits are just as good (and a lot safer) as one big one.

6. **Use only money that you can afford to lose.** While you might borrow for investment (or do the sharemarket equivalent of buying options and warrants), short-term trading should be done with your own money. That should be money that is not earmarked for next year's taxes or your savings for an overseas trip.

7. **Cut your losses.** You will make mistakes – don't let them be too costly. If your purchase is not rising as expected, get out and find another opportunity.

8. **It is as easy to sell as to buy.** It is also nearly as easy to sell as it is to hold. One call to a broker (or a few clicks on the Internet) is all it takes to close out your position. Don't forget that in

some markets you can trade by taking a negative position and selling short.

9. **Be informed.** A lot of success in trading is about having plenty of good information.

10. **Be patient.** People may tell you of the great profits that they've made in a few days – but it's rare. You may have to wait for months, even a year or two, for a takeover to happen. However, it's worth waiting for if the shares that you bought at 220c get bought out at 280c – that's a 27% profit, a lot better than most other things that you would have your money in.

WAY FOUR

Get offshore

The fall in offshore sharemarkets in the early 2000s and again in 2008–2009 (especially in the USA) hurt a lot of Kiwi investors. So many of us have been encouraged to get money into global markets – the need to diversify and the profits that were available being particularly compelling arguments. Anyone who had been invested offshore through the 1990s will have done very well. However, at the end of 2000, a good amount of the profits were given back as markets fell by 50% or more in some cases. The same is mostly true for the 2000s – following the dot-com crash there were good profits from share investment although the markets never reached their previous highs.

The need to get offshore is still compelling. You should not let what has happened to the markets put you off. Even though there is greater correlation between markets and they increasingly move in unison, you still get diversification from offshore sharemarkets – getting money offshore reduces risk. There will still be profits offshore – since the crash in the early 2000s, the sharemarkets bounced upwards strongly and did so again in 2009. You still need to avail yourself of the opportunities that other markets offer.

One of the questions that I ask my WealthCoaching clients is: 'What would the performance of your portfolio be if New Zealand got foot-and-mouth disease?' This often sends people shaking uncontrollably at the thought – New Zealand is a small and brittle economy: something like foot-and-mouth disease (or some other economic calamity) would devastate it. Only those who had offshore investments would cope with the consequences.

There will always be ups and downs in the global economies. Just because there is an economic slowdown (or recession) does not mean that the long-term upward sweep of the markets is finished. There is an explosion in the amount of human knowledge, in technology (not just in computers and software but also in things like pharmaceuticals, textiles, biotechnology, agriculture and medicine), and in our ways of doing things and managing businesses. Our way of living, our society and our economic organisations are changing rapidly. Everything must be done so much more quickly (time is invaluable) and yet, seemingly a paradox, leisure as an industry is a major growth area.

Brands have become critical. Children clamour for the stuff that McDonald's offers; a label turns an ordinary tee shirt worth $20 into one with a price tag of $70; Coca Cola did not win the taste test but has much higher sales and margins than Pepsi. Brands matter!

On top of all of this, the Internet has changed everything. It will continue to develop, continue to change the way we do business, and continue to make some people rich. Google seems to me to be a good example of a new way of making money on the Internet. It will not be the last.

New Zealand is not completely devoid of these things. We do have companies developing technologies; we do have companies that are using computers and technology to make their businesses more efficient and more profitable. However, we do not have major global brands; we do not have major pharmaceutical or biotechnology companies; we do not have many investments at the cutting edge of major new developments. To get

We do not have . . . major pharmaceutical or biotechnology companies; we do not have many investments at the cutting edge of major new developments.

into these things, you must have money offshore.

All of these things, the Internet, new technological developments and changes, growth of brands and new lifestyles, are opportunities for riches. The shifts in our ways of doing things, the development of technology and the Internet will see a transfer of wealth from one group to another. That happened during the Industrial Revolution but what is happening today makes the Industrial Revolution pale into insignificance.

OLD INDUSTRIES ARE OKAY!

This is not to completely denigrate or ignore shares in businesses which operate in more traditional industries. Smart investors do not only go into new industries. Many older industries have performed well and will continue to do well as they provide their goods and services to a continuing strong market. Those with strong management and direction will benefit from technological growth as they use new computers, software and database management systems to bring efficiencies. Good companies, in whatever industry, will embrace new management systems, use technology and adopt best practice in all of their areas of operation. Such things ultimately increase sales and cut costs – and help smart companies with smart managers make more money for their smart shareholders and investors.

In fact, some of the oldest industries will be the greatest beneficiaries of the changes that are happening. Medicine and banking are old industries. But both have seized technology and are using it to create efficiencies and advance their practices to make money. Both are also very targeted at the baby boomers – that huge cohort which is now getting into middle age and demanding better healthcare and financial services. It is hard to see the growth in these two industries slowing down.

To participate in this explosion of growth you must be in offshore equities.

To participate in this explosion of growth you must be in offshore equities.

You cannot enjoy the profits from the next Viagra or Lipitor by having your money in the bank; you cannot profit from selling financial services to anxious baby boomers by having your money in Dunedin City Council stock. To profit from pharmaceuticals or financial services, software development or services to tourists, you must own shares. There is no alternative.

A GOOD TIME TO BUY?

Is this a good time to buy global shares? Provided that you are going into the market for the long haul, the answer to that must be an emphatic yes. These are great times for investors. Although shares around the world are not at bargain prices, there are good growth prospects – the fall in share prices in 2008–2009 has got rid of a lot of dross, forced companies to report more accurately and honestly and therefore reduced a lot of the risk for investors.

The economic growth in China and India is creating consumer societies in both countries (India has the biggest middle class in the world). There are many opportunities at the moment for businesses to enter new markets and sell to new customers. One day the growth that we are currently enjoying will end – but with the exception of the usual cyclical slowdowns and recessions, I do not see the overall upward trend ending at the moment.

> Discontinuity creates huge opportunities but also presents substantial threats to existing businesses and industries.

OFFSHORE INVESTMENT IS GETTING EASY

There are now no impediments to investing offshore. The only thing stopping you is the blinkers that you have put on yourself. It is easy to transfer foreign currency, sharebrokers will recommend shares for you, fund managers have specialist unit trusts, information is freely available on the Internet . . . there is nothing to hinder you.

In spite of this, the more things change, the more they stay the same. Share investment is about buying into businesses that make good profits which will grow. That has always been the case and it will always be the case. Regardless of whether the company invents new microprocessors, discovers new drugs, publishes newspapers or grows pine trees, it is the sustainable cashflow from the company's assets which gives its shares value. Start-up companies have high prices because investors see huge profits coming one day (even though they may have none at the moment). The driver for share price growth remains the same regardless of the industry. That driver is profits.

I do not know what will happen in the next year or two on the sharemarkets. In America, the economy and markets are still fairly highly valued and there is still a great deal of indebtedness. There will have to be more 'de-leveraging' and, with many governments carrying huge debt there is a high risk of inflation. In my view, there is still a great deal of risk to equity markets.

However, I do believe the great bull run of the 20th century will remain intact well into the 21st century. There could be more downs, perhaps quite substantial downs. However, over time these downs will be overtaken by the ups. It may take some patience and strong nerves but owning a share of a good business will continue to be a profitable exercise.

The shakeouts which happen over the years should be greeted by the genuine investor enthusiastically. While all shares are harshly treated by the market at such times, good companies are only temporarily affected. It is those who have no sales, no profits and not much in the way of a business which are hammered down and which stay down. Big falls in the market have a very good sorting effect – the cold wind that blows through the market gets rid of the chaff, leaving the oats. The dross that is blown away by market shakeouts is only ever missed by those silly enough to be 'invested' in it.

It is hard to believe that 21st-century people will lose their way and stop inventing things. It is hard to see technological growth stopping. It is hard to see us losing our knowledge and the momentum of our drive for more knowledge. It is hard to see especially a slowing (let alone a cessation) of the development of new health products and drugs. Indeed, it seems obvious that the growth in our knowledge, in our technology and especially in things which will improve our health, will increase not decrease.

The overall thrust in change in computers, software, pharmaceuticals, agriculture and the like will continue. And they will take economies along with them. You can be a part of it all, whether by buying the tech companies themselves, the companies that supply the tech companies or companies that benefit from technology. But there is only one way to benefit: by buying shares.

The overall thrust in change in computers, software, pharmaceuticals, agriculture and the like will continue.

Just about everyone has at least some offshore investments now – Kiwis have poured billions of dollars into overseas shares, property and unit trusts since exchange restrictions were removed 25 years ago. They have been encouraged to do that, quite rightly, by investment advisers, financial planners, fund managers and sharebrokers. Regrettably they have also been sold offshore investments that have not turned out so well – Gold Coast property (often bought sight unseen) and obscure shares sold by enthusiastic brokers phoning from Bangkok.

IN DEFENCE OF THE NEW ZEALAND MARKET

I do not believe that the New Zealand sharemarket is a dog – in fact it has presented investors with some very good opportunities over the last decade or so: Telecom, The Warehouse, Rakon, Auckland International Airport, Sky TV, Infratil, Fletcher Building, Ryman, Michael Hill . . . the shareholders in these companies have barked all right, laughing all the way to the bank. The market has not bounced back from the Great Recession as well as some others. Nevertheless, our market does provide a higher dividend yield than others and has shown good growth as well. I think the New Zealand market has provided, and will continue to provide, good opportunities.

Nevertheless, you do need to get a significant proportion of your investment funds offshore – probably 40–60% should be overseas. The reasons for investing offshore have been well covered in the media for years. Very briefly, the major ones are:

- Offshore investment opens up a whole new range of opportunities. The New Zealand sharemarket makes up less than half of 1% of the total world markets. If you limited yourself to New Zealand, you would be closing yourself off from over 99% of the opportunities that are available.
- You can get into industries that New Zealand does not have, e.g. pharmaceuticals, banks and textiles.
- You diversify your investments, spreading your risk around the globe. This is still valid, even though many people have pointed out that the correlation between markets around the world is now quite close. New Zealand is a small and quite brittle economy.
- You can invest in major global brands. New Zealand has some strong brands (Pumpkin Patch and Michael Hill are good brands) but they pale into insignificance compared to Coca Cola, American Express, Intel, etc.
- Foreign currency hedge. Holding offshore investments guards against a fall in the New Zealand dollar, which is particularly important for those who travel a lot. This, of course, can be a double-edged sword – a rise in the New Zealand dollar can quickly wipe out investment gains made overseas. However, at the time of writing, the current level of the New Zealand dollar seems to make it a very good time to put money offshore.

If you go about offshore investment in the right way, it will have a major impact on your investment performance. You may have the bulk of your money in the New Zealand market and will almost certainly do your short-term trades here, but the greater opportunities available, coupled with the likely higher long-term performance in offshore markets, make it essential to get some money offshore.

> **If you go about offshore investment in the right way, it will have a major impact on your investment performance.**

Offshore investment does have some disadvantages:

- **Tax.** Dividends from offshore investments do not come with imputation credits. This means that you will pay tax on the dividend you receive even though the company has already paid tax. This double taxation eats into returns and applies to all countries, even Australia.

  In some ways the new legislation regarding foreign investment and which applies to all countries outside of Australia has mitigated the double taxation of investments. This is the 'deemed dividend' scheme which came into effect in April 2007. The basic principle is that those who have offshore investments over $50,000 will be deemed to be receiving a dividend of 5% whether they receive such dividends or not. Therefore, you will be assumed to have income equivalent to 5% of your investment holdings and will be taxed on this. Most overseas companies do not at present pay dividends of anywhere near 5% and so there is a component of a tax on unrealised capital gains.

  Nevertheless, dividends that you receive are not taxed and so there are investments where this scheme actually leaves you better off – i.e. where an investment pays a dividend greater than 5%. Australian dividends continue to be double taxed because Australia is outside these rules. While many of us with offshore holdings dislike this tax because of the greater compliance costs, you must remember that there is a basic rule of investing which says that you do not invest solely on the basis of tax. You should first work out what is a good investment – the way that it is taxed is secondary. With this in mind, I think that people should continue to invest offshore even though they will be subject to this new tax.

- **Foreign exchange.** While this can be an advantage of investing offshore, it can also be a disadvantage if the currency moves the wrong way. Over the long term (years and decades) this may work itself out – your returns should offset adverse currency movement, if that's what happens. In any event, it is quite probable that the strong economies in which you are investing will have stronger currencies than New Zealand's. However, in the short term currency movements may seriously erode your returns.

  Picking likely future currency movements varies from extremely difficult to impossible (this is especially so for short-term currency movements). My advice is to invest offshore for the long term in countries that you are likely to visit regularly. This provides a natural hedge: if you invest in the UK, you will still be able to afford a night in a decent London hotel without having to raise a mortgage – regardless of what Sterling does.

- **Information.** It is certainly easier to get information on offshore investments than it once was. The Internet will give you real-time share prices, company news, financials, charts, etc. You can also find out easily enough about the economy, industries that you are interested in, the legal and tax environment and politics. However, what most of us miss out on is an idea of trends and what is likely to happen in the future. That requires living there, talking to ordinary people, a network of contacts. It is hard to get these things if you are not there on the ground.

These disadvantages are not a worry if you only invest in New Zealand. We have one of the most investor-friendly tax regimes (no capital gains tax and imputation credits), there is no foreign exchange risk and information is plentiful and understandable. Tempting though it may be at times to invest only in New Zealand, I reiterate that you should get a substantial portion of your portfolio offshore.

EMERGING MARKETS VERSUS MATURE MARKETS

Perhaps one of the most fundamental choices that you have to make regarding your offshore investments is whether to go into emerging markets or into more mature and developed economies.

Emerging markets	Mature markets
Latin America	Europe
Asia - China	
- India	USA
- Thailand	Canada
- Korea, etc.	UK
Eastern Europe	Japan
- Turkey	
- Greece	
- Russia	

Overall, emerging economies are likely to have greater growth in GDP (that's why they are emerging). As such they can present exciting though volatile and risky investments. With the ease with which investors and institutions can shift capital around the world, money will soon flow into an erstwhile moribund economy when it starts to grow. Emerging markets have certainly made for very profitable investing over the last decade or so; coming off a low base they can give explosive investment returns. BRIC countries (Brazil, Russia, India and China) have been especially profitable.

However, they *are* risky. That same smart money that moves in rapidly will leave just as quickly. International investors are flighty and will run if the economy turns down, the currency looks vulnerable, there is political change or any number of other things. The risks involved in emerging markets make it essential to buy into not just one country but a spread. Even that may not completely shed risk – the Asian crisis of 1997 affected nearly all Asian countries. Nevertheless, a spread of countries and regions will cut risk to some extent.

MATURE MARKETS

Overall, these will not give the same returns nor carry the same risk as emerging markets. Mature markets will not see explosive growth (although there are certainly exceptions) because they need to come off a high base. P:E ratios are generally higher in mature markets – these higher P:E ratios might be several times the nearest equivalent in a developing country and reflect the solid, established nature of the companies as well as the very low country risk (it's hard to imagine a *coup d'état* in Switzerland, but not so hard to imagine one in Turkey).

> The risks involved in emerging markets make it essential to buy into not just one country but a spread.

There is nothing to stop you going into emerging markets as well as trying to pick a few winners from mature markets – indeed, that is probably a very sensible strategy. Nevertheless, most people tend one way or the other, gravitating towards their natural inclination.

HOW MUCH OFFSHORE?

This depends on a range of factors, in part at least on your personal circumstances:

- Do you travel a lot? If you do, you need offshore investments as a hedge. In addition, travelling a lot will give you a good feel for the investment climate which should encourage you to put more money overseas.
- Do you have good offshore contacts? If you do (perhaps through your job or business or because you are an immigrant), you should have more confidence to put money offshore.
- Are you an importer or reliant on imports? If so, put money offshore as a natural hedge.
- Do you believe the New Zealand economy will underperform other economies? If so, shift a higher proportion of your money to where you think it will perform.

SKINNING CATS

I'm told that there are lots of ways to skin a cat (I'll have to take that at face value – I've never tried). However, I do know that there are lots of ways to get exposure to offshore markets and investments. In fact the choice is so great, many people wonder how to start or even don't start. The array of offshore investments available gives you every right to feel confused.

There are two main options in choosing how to get your money offshore:

1. Direct investment.
2. Indirect investment through companies and managed funds.

DIRECT OFFSHORE INVESTMENT

This simply means buying individual shares in companies that are registered overseas. Usually (although not always) you will buy these shares on the stock exchange of the country concerned.

There are some companies that you can buy on the New Zealand Stock Exchange which are predominantly offshore companies. These are companies that have dual listing – they were originally listed on their home country's exchange but because they have had a lot of assets and quite a few investors from our country, they have arranged to be listed on the New Zealand market as well. Companies like AMP, Telstra and Westpac Bank all have their primary listing in Australia but are also listed on the New Zealand Stock Exchange.

Buying these companies is just like buying any company on the New Zealand market. The price will be very similar to the price in Australia after the exchange rate has been calculated. The company will be registered in Australia and so your shareholding will be with an Australian share registry office and the dividends that you receive will come in Australian dollars. You have bought an Australian company whose shares just happen to be listed on the New Zealand Stock Exchange. The company is therefore subject to Australian tax and regulatory law. Your money is invested largely in Australian assets. These companies that have dual listings may have small parts of their business here in New Zealand but the bulk is in Australia.

Even if your target company does not have a dual listing, it is still very easy to buy Australian shares. All of the big sharebrokers have offices in Australia and any broker that does not will have an agent there who will arrange the buying and selling on your behalf. The broker will also arrange your foreign currency for you, meaning that you need only write a New Zealand cheque to pay for your shares.

Once you own Australian shares it is very easy to keep abreast of what is happening. Most newspapers have quite good Australian share tables and often report Australian business news; there is the Internet with dozens of sites for investors; some tip sheets have Australian sections and most brokers make recommendations on Australian shares. Australian share investing is little different from investing here.

BEYOND AUSTRALIA

However, Australia by global standards is really quite small and limited in opportunities. In fact, Australians are exhorted to get money offshore every bit as much as we are. Australia does give New Zealanders diversification into industries that we don't have (banks and mining in particular), which gives good exposure to Asia. However, to really diversify and to get into cutting-edge industries and into companies with global brands, you need to go beyond Australasia.

There is nothing technically stopping you from making direct equity investments anywhere you want in the world. While I only seldom buy shares directly outside Australasia, I know many people who have shares in places such as UK, Singapore, Canada, Ireland, USA and Hong Kong. The only impediment to investing in these countries is working out what to buy. All are English-speaking and have reasonably open economies. While you might struggle to get a feel for the economic and business climate, which may make investment decisions a bit difficult, you can if you want, invest simply by making a call to your broker who will arrange the sale or purchase for you and the foreign exchange.

Outside of these countries is more problematical. English is not a universal language and that in itself may create problems. The Czech Republic may have some very attractive opportunities, particularly since it has joined the EU, but have you ever tried reading a Czech annual report or dividend statement? Former Eastern Bloc countries and Asian countries like China, Thailand, Indonesia, India, Vietnam and Korea may have some very good investments, but unless you understand the language, the culture and the business environment you are probably better to forget direct investment and go in through managed funds.

GO CANNY

Go into all direct foreign investments very carefully. This is certainly an area where you should start with a small amount of money and add to it as you gain knowledge, experience and confidence. On the whole you should stick to heavyweight companies in growth industries. Think long term like an investor rather than short term like a trader. Pick the industry that you find attractive (e.g. construction) and then go into the companies that are market leaders. You can do well on the New Zealand market with companies that are in poorly performing industries. However, this is through good local knowledge, something you do not have when investing offshore.

OFFSHORE BROKERS

If you are going to invest directly into overseas shares you must choose whether to use a New Zealand broker or an offshore one. Using a New Zealand broker is certainly more convenient. Most of the larger New Zealand brokers are branches of overseas brokers and so have offices around the world. You will already have a relationship with your New Zealand broker, who can buy and sell for you using the office in the country in which you invest. Even the smaller brokers have relationships with overseas brokers who act as agents. Using a New Zealand broker will probably cost more as there is often brokerage to pay to both the New Zealand broker and the overseas one. People who are buying and selling a lot offshore will probably want to set up an account with an overseas broker. Choose a larger, reputable one who can provide you with good research and information.

Be very wary of brokers emailing and calling from overseas with a 'hot' deal. I know people who have lost substantial amounts of money this way. The companies that these brokers recommend are almost all small, obscure and speculative. If they were such a good investment the shares would be easy enough for the broker to shift in their own country – they shouldn't have to make a phone call to the other end of the earth. Some of these shares have been warehoused: the brokers have bought a large quantity of shares very cheaply and then go out and sell them at a profit. While I have had dozens of phone calls offering shares, I have never taken them up, preferring instead to stay in the mainstream.

> Be very wary of brokers calling from overseas with a 'hot' deal.

INDIRECT OFFSHORE INVESTMENT

If you do not want to buy shares directly offshore yourself, there are still some great opportunities through a whole range of vehicles. You can very easily get exposure to offshore economies and industries through other means. Most of these are managed funds of one sort or another.

NEW ZEALAND SHARES

However, before looking at the different types of managed funds, it is worth noting that many New Zealand companies now have a proportion of their business assets offshore. Michael Hill, Pumpkin Patch, Infratil, GPG, Tourism Holdings and many others have significant operations in Australia and elsewhere.

Owning any one of these companies gives you exposure to

overseas businesses. It may not be as much offshore exposure nor into the particular industry that you want, but it does nevertheless increase your diversification beyond the New Zealand economy.

OFFSHORE INVESTMENT THROUGH MANAGED FUNDS

There are a lot of different types of managed funds. However, what they all have in common is that investors' funds are pooled, then given to a manager who invests and manages them in areas which have been agreed and according to the rules set out in advance. Obviously this manager charges for its service, usually an amount according to the size of the fund and its performance.

There are several broad types of managed funds:

UNIT TRUSTS

These are the usual open-ended funds that are offered by nearly every bank, insurance company and fund manager in the country and which are sold by the likes of financial planners and investment advisers. They are called 'open' because there is not a set number of units that can be issued. The fund manager will keep issuing units as fast as its network of brokers and advisers can sell them, and if you want to cash up, the fund manager will redeem your units from the fund. In this way, the number of units on issue can fluctuate considerably.

There are unit trusts available to give you exposure to just about any market (and therefore any economy) that you can think of. You can buy into unit trusts that are based on Japan or Korea, unit trusts based on emerging markets or technology or energy, etc. These unit trusts are actively managed. This means that the manager tries to pick winners, companies that will outperform, and buys and sells regularly. Sometimes the manager will hand over stock selection to someone else. This is usually when the manager does not have an office or staff in the country on which the fund is based. Instead of stock picking from afar, the manager will appoint a specialist equity analysis and fund management company in that country and charge it with using its local knowledge to pick the right stocks.

Unit trusts may offer good differentiation and targeting of particular countries and investment areas, but they do have the drawback that the fees that are charged tend to be quite high. The costs associated with active stock picking are high and so these costs are passed on to the unit holder. Nevertheless, some of these funds have done spectacularly well. They have taken advantage of booming offshore markets and rewarded their investors handsomely.

> **There are unit trusts available to give you exposure to just about any market.**

PASSIVE INDEX TRACKER

There is really only one of these which is based on offshore equities and which is listed on the New Zealand sharemarket, and that is WiNZ. WiNZ is an index tracker which tracks the World Index. As such it gives you at least some exposure to all of the major sharemarkets in the world. The World Index is made up of shares from right around the world in proportion to the market capitalisation of the companies and so represents a benchmark for global share performance.

WiNZ tracks this index and is listed on the New Zealand sharemarket so that you can very easily buy units and make a very broad-based, diversified investment. As an investment it has performed very well when the markets have boomed and very badly when they have fallen.The manager of WiNZ values the units of the fund each day and announces this to the market. The units trade on the market at a level very close to this value. Because the fund is passively managed (it's done largely by computer) the management fees are relatively low. The only cost of buying and selling units is brokerage (your sharebroker will charge the same to buy or sell WiNZ units as he or she would charge for any share on the market). WiNZ is tax efficient, as being a passive fund there is no capital gains tax to pay.

The problem with WiNZ is that there is no targeting of particularly favourable investment areas. You get exposure to all the world's markets according to their size (which makes the USA the biggest part of WiNZ). However, it can form a good base for your offshore exposure, a good diversified global holding into which you can put the bulk of your overseas money while using the balance to target areas that you think might be especially good. WiNZ, or something like it, can act as your core holding for perhaps 50–70% of your overseas funds, allowing you then to pick a few specialist stocks or funds in areas that you particularly like.

Many investors want to get more specific than simply buying the World Index. For example, you may want to overweight your portfolio to Korea or to US healthcare or to silver or telecommunications ... An easy way to do this is through iShares (***www.ishares.com***). These are passive funds that are listed on various stock exchanges around the world (most are in the USA) and which track a very wide range of indices based on industries (technology, biotechnology, natural resources, finance, transport, etc) or countries (Turkey, Eastern Europe, South Africa, Taiwan, etc). Any New Zealand broker will be able to buy these for you.

WAY FIVE

Be informed

Predicting the future is hard. Many have tried it, using all sorts of systems, most with only limited success. And yet when you invest, that is what you are doing: you are predicting what you think will happen to a company and then staking your money on that prediction. Having to back your predictions of the future with your money should sound scary – it is scary. But if you are going to make investments (any investments), that is what you have to do.

For many, putting cash on the line is the difficult part. Most of us are quite happy to make predictions when our money is not at risk – when money which has (possibly) been hard-earned is at stake things are harder. I have often heard advisers suggest to new investors or traders that they 'practise' before they start for real. This means pretending to make a purchase without going ahead and calling a broker to place an order. This might help a bit, but really it is too easy. It is a big step from practising to committing yourself and your money.

> The best investors are those who make the best predictions.

The best investors are those who make the best predictions. To beat the market, you have to make predictions which are better than average. How are you going to predict what and how a company will do and what and how the market will perform?

There are essentially two ways of making buy or sell decisions:

1. Technical analysis.
2. Fundamental analysis.

TECHNICAL ANALYSIS

Technical analysis is a means of predicting the future and therefore helping with buy/sell decisions. It involves looking at graphs and charts to find patterns that will repeat themselves. Although I do not use it myself I know people who do and these are people who are serious about the sharemarket.

I don't use technical analysis because I am mostly an investor. Technical analysis may have some use for traders but its use to long-term investors is limited. Technical analysis might be able to tell you the short-term movements of a market but it does not give your earnings growth, P:E ratios, dividend yields, etc.

People who do technical analysis are called chartists (because they draw charts). The basic idea is that they are looking for trends. These trends come from crowd behaviour and psychology as large numbers of people make decisions and push the market one way or another. The theory is to graph (or chart) the movements of the market to more easily see the trends. These charts show patterns that are recognisable from past market behaviours and so give clues to the future of the market.

There are several different forms of graphs that are used and these have spawned an incredible amount of jargon. There are wedges, pennants, exhaustion gaps, moving averages, breakouts, stochastic oscillators, head and shoulders, Japanese candlesticks, breakaway gaps, Fibonacci sequences, impulse waves, Bollinger bands ... to hear two chartists talking to each other is like listening to NASA scientists. I have no intention to even try to explain these things. If you are serious about trading and want to use technical analysis, there are specialist books written by people far more expert than I am.

It struck me about 30 years ago, when Elliott Wave theory

had some currency (Elliott Wave theory is a branch of technical analysis) that you would need to be very keen on trading as opposed to investing to learn this stuff. There is a great deal to absorb just to be able to speak the language properly, let alone use it to trade successfully. I have never been that interested in trading so have not put in the time. If you want to become a serious share trader you should make the effort to learn it properly and thoroughly (it may take years) because it will probably help a bit in your trading. In particular, study the use of moving averages which appear to me to be the most useful. If you are going to be mostly an investor rather than a trader, then forget it.

COMPUTER-BASED CHARTING

Some organisations have been offering computer programs along with training in how to use them as a means of making buy and sell decisions. The programs with training are expensive (up to $10,000). This cost puts them outside the use of the majority of sharemarket investors.

I am fairly sceptical of these offerings. First, you would have to be very sure that you were going to want to do a lot of serious trading to make the time and money spent worthwhile. Second, the programmes are only going to be as good as the underlying charting philosophy and system. I've never thought that charting and technical analysis were terribly good. Third, I do not believe that any system can be followed slavishly and without thought. Some of these systems have produced results that are self-fufilling – that is, they have enough people using their systems to push the market price of a share when a buy or sell recommendation is made by the programme. At best, charting represents an indicator as to what you should do. If you are a big and frequent trader, computer programs will be another tool in the box. If not, forget them. Don't dabble with charting – either learn it properly and use it or don't bother with it.

I've never thought that charting and technical analysis were terribly good.

FUNDAMENTAL ANALYSIS

The best way to predict the future is to collect information, study it and think. 'Study' is an ugly word with connotations of schooldays. Well, this was never going to be a cakewalk. Fundamental analysis involves looking at the fundamentals of companies and their businesses. It means accumulating information on assets and earning, and understanding how companies run their businesses. To beat the market you need to know and understand your target business, in particular, what is important and what is not.

The people who beat the market are those with:

- The most information.
- The best information.
- The most useful information.

All three of these are satisfied by having inside information. However, that is hard to get for most of us and, anyway, even if you had it, it is illegal and immoral to use. Having said that, insider trading happens frequently and those who do use privileged information can reap great profits. If you look back at events you can easily see that the price started to move before any public announcement is made. Insider trading can now be a criminal offence. Previously it was a civil matter to be litigated between parties.

BASIC INFORMATION

Much of the information that you need is easy to get. You need to know things like:

- The number of shares on issue.
- The names of the directors.
- Financials (previous years' profits, assets and liabilities).
- Major shareholders.

As well as this you need to be able to predict future profitability (see below). Before you can start to do any sort of fundamental analysis you need this sort of basic information. Much of this can usually be obtained on your target's own website. Most companies have a section 'about us' which provides much of the basic information that you need.

ANNUAL REPORT

All of the basic information comes in the company's annual report (and other interim reports). These are full of information, and along with basic information contain a statement from the board of directors about the last period's business activities and usually a pointer to the future. Of course, the predictions of the future from the chairman in a report to shareholders is seldom pessimistic and so has to be read with due scepticism.

Once you are a shareholder in a company, you will receive these reports or you can get them on-line from the company's own website. Many people buy a few shares in companies that they are interested in just to make sure they get the reports, although I find it easier to go to the 'investor' section of the company's website and get the annual report from there.

The most important part of the annual report is the company's accounts and financial statements. These will have already been announced to the public via the news media but there is a great deal of detail found in the accounts in the annual report which is always interesting. In particular are the notes to the accounts which give much detail on the company's activity and finances. While the appearance of these accounts can be quite daunting, this fine print should all be read. It helps to have financial skill to read them properly, though much of the material contained can be understood well enough with a good application of common sense.

You must, however, be careful with annual reports because they are often out of date. The report will be attributed a certain date (e.g. 30 June) and this date can be some months before the report is sent out. To work out P:E ratios you need to be sure that the number of shares on issue is accurate. While the annual report will tell you this figure as it was when the report was published, shares on issue can change: there may have been new shares through bonus or cash issues, staff options to buy shares may have been exercised, or shares might be issued to acquire a new business. It may even be that the company has bought back and cancelled some of its own shares and so the shares on issue are less than in the most recent reports. A full-service share-broker should be able to tell you the number of shares on issue at any particular time and if you are in any doubt you could try phoning the share registry office that the company uses (I have done this successfully in the past).

YEAR BOOKS

As well as annual reports from companies, the *Investment Year Book* is available to give you a lot of basic information such as shares on issue, directors, financial summary for the last five years, dividends paid, a graph of the share price, brokers' profit forecasts, contact details of the company, share registry, new issues of shares, major shareholders and a half page of comments. No serious investor would be without an *Investment Year Book* – it is available from Investment Research Group, PO Box 30-988, Lower Hutt.

ON-LINE

Although the *Year Books* are good, they also quickly become out of date. They are printed annually and a lot can happen over the course of a year (new shares issued, resignation or appointment of directors, sale of major assets, etc). You can get more up-to-date basic information by going on-line. The NZX has a website with much of this basic information and also gives the announcements that companies make to the NZX from time to time.

NEWSPAPERS

The daily newspaper and the weeklies like the *Sunday Star Times*, *National Business Review* and the *Independent* have an importance for investors in that they give news and comment on what is happening – both on the sharemarket itself and in relation to what companies are doing. They also have a role through their share tables in giving the latest sales on the market and financial information like P:E ratios, dividend yields, etc.

Although newspapers do a good job giving share prices, the financial ratios that they give are not to be trusted.

Although newspapers do a good job giving news, the financial ratios that they give are not to be trusted. You cannot rely on the newspaper share tables for P:E ratios, dividend yields or net tangible asset backing. This is for two reasons:

1. The financials are sometimes calculated straight from the company's financial report and sometimes not adjusted for any extraordinary items. This may see a company shown as selling on a particularly low P:E. That extraordinary profit is unlikely to recur, meaning its ongoing P:E will be substantially higher. Similarly with net asset backing – this may look very low because the nta is only stated at book value rather than market value. You cannot blame the newspapers for these discrepancies – their tables have to be based on the official financial reports. Nevertheless, you must be wary of them and never rely completely on such figures.

2. The newspapers' share tables give historic financials. Therefore the P:Es, ntas and dividend yields are based on the previous year's financials, not the current year, let alone future years. Use newspapers to get share prices and company news, but only use them for financial ratios as a starting point. The ratios that are listed in share tables might give you a point from which to do further investigation but no more than that.

The newspapers, annual reports, NZX, Findata and the *Investment Year Book* will, along with a broker's research and on-line access, give good basic information. You do need this – to predict the future you need to know accurately where things are at the moment. However, to assess where companies are going, what will be good and what will be bad, you need much more information. Often this information needs to be pieced together from different sources, little snippets added together to get the full picture.

PREDICTING PROFIT GROWTH

This is the key to successful share investing. If you could know that a company was going to increase its profits substantially over the next few years (or indeed if you knew the profits were going to decline) you would act accordingly.

The companies themselves of course will have a good idea what they are going to make in the future. They know how they are doing right now and have budgets and plans for the next few years (although things do not always go to plan). Under the 'continuous disclosure' rules of the NZX, companies now have an obligation to disclose information that might affect the share price. This includes financial projection where such projections are at variance with the market's forecasts. This is on the basis that this information belongs to all shareholders and therefore should be available to all. Companies disclose this information to the NZX and the NZX puts it on its website (***www.nzx.com***).

To get an indication of longer-term projections, you need to do two things:

1. Look at brokers' reports and tip sheets.

2. Keep abreast of what is going on.

BROKERS' REPORTS

Brokers have two advantages. First, they have trained investment analysts who spend their entire working days analysing companies. The big firms will have an analyst who is responsible for a few companies and becomes expert on those companies and the areas in which they operate. For example, one analyst will be responsible for keeping abreast of what is going on in retail or tourism. Second, the brokers and their analysts invite themselves to companies, visit with management and talk to them about what is happening in the business. The analyst is trying to get to know the company and its operations as well as he or she can. The broker should wear a black hat during this exercise – the company will try to put a positive spin on everything that it is doing and won't share any dark secrets that it might have. Nevertheless, the broker's analyst gets far more information than a private investor would ever get. The analyst can use this by looking at each of the components of the business to predict future earnings. The brokers then disseminate the results of their analysis to their clients, along with a recommendation.

This makes brokers' research bulletins and newsletters essential reading for you. The bigger brokers put out book-size reports, which cover perhaps 30 or more companies, and then update these electronically as the need arises. The brokers are not always right, of course – business analysis is not a precise science; predicting the future is not easy for a sharebroker either! However, you should make sure that you get as many reports from different brokers as you can on any company in which you are interested.

The broker's analyst gets far more information than a private investor would ever get.

I receive a couple of email updates from my brokers each day: one for New Zealand and the other for Australia. They also send me monthly research by email and if I am interested in a company they will send the research that they have.

TIP SHEETS

Tip sheets are regular newsletters that you can get on a subscription basis. Tip sheets have come and gone over the years – they proliferate during good times and all but a few disappear in bad times.

It would be reasonable to think that much of the content of some tip sheets comes from brokers – I am sure it does. Nevertheless, even if the tip sheet compiler did nothing more than read everything that all the brokers put out and applied common sense to filter out the rubbish, they would provide a useful service. Most, however, do more than that, with company visits (or at least phone calls), and they obviously get enough information around the markets to make reasonable predictions.

My worry about tip sheets is that, like brokers, they are too optimistic and put out too many 'buy' recommendations without warning off their readers from the outstanding junk which is often overhyped. Presumably they find that 'buy' recommendations sell subscriptions better – or are the tip sheet editors not very keen on insulting companies?

KEEPING ABREAST

Top investors have very inquisitive personalities – they need to know what is going on. They keep up with trends in the world, in the economy, in various industries and in particular companies. To beat the market you need to be alert to everything that is happening, continuously asking yourself how events will affect companies in which you have an interest. Knowing what is going on means using the news media in all of their various forms. Running through this is the attitude of ownership. The companies in which you are invested are *your* companies (in part) and you should be trying to find out as much as you can about the businesses that you own.

Remember always that share investing means looking for businesses that are making exceptional profits and will grow those profits and keep on growing them over long periods of time.

To beat the market, you are looking for businesses that will do better in terms of profit growth than other ones. In effect, you want information that will tell you how a business is likely to do. Some of this is gained from watching what is happening and applying plain common sense. For example, Warren Buffett likes Coca Cola as a company because he knows that any retailer who sells soft drinks has to have that brand. In New Zealand you can watch a business like Michael Hill grow and prosper, and see its shops full of customers.

NEWS MEDIA

While many investors use newspapers (daily and weekly) to learn what is happening on the market, their use extends far beyond that. Newspapers are probably the best source of business and company news, both in terms of reporting events and for commentary. The good thing about newspapers is that information in them is permanent (unlike radio and television). It is easy to clip an article and file it so that it is available for future reference.

The trouble with clipping articles is that after a year or two you can have a mountain of stuff and, if it is not well filed, it can be hard to find and use again in the future. At one time, I kept every copy of *National Business Review* as a record of what had happened. I ended up with a pile a metre high which was too daunting to ever go into. The *NBRs* were eventually filed in the wheelie bin.

Now I use my computer to record basic information like company announcements and reports to the stock exchange. In addition, I copy articles and file them – I have a file for each company that I am interested in. While newspapers are a primary source of what is going on, investors should not ignore radio either. National Radio has business and market reports at 6.45 a.m. (which I find very good) as well as another at 12.15 p.m. The one at 12.15 is often a repeat of the morning stories but has a broker's report on the morning's trade. There are other business programmes on the radio which are no doubt worth listening to. Radio provides no permanent record, but it does have an immediacy that is good.

ON-LINE

Many investors get most of their information on-line. They store it there too. The Internet gives you rapid information and lots of it, with no filing of paper.

As stated above, I use ***findata.co.nz*** for much of the basic information that I need. I keep my portfolio on it and it tells me how this is doing instantly as well as 'real-time' share prices. I go into it at least twice a day to see what is happening, pick up company news and to see how that news has affected share prices.

For someone living in Queenstown, where the local paper is *Mountain Scene*, I think that's great. The other site that I find very good is ***www.sharechat.co.nz***. I get about 10 emails each day from them with news (almost) as it happens. This is a free site, and the 'alerts' are also free – well worth bookmarking and using their 'share alert' service.

You should also not ignore the NZX's own site (***www.nzx.com***). This has a lot of information including company announcements, share prices and links through to companies and brokers.

OFFSHORE

Perhaps the best thing about the Internet is the ease with which you can keep abreast of what is happening around the globe. You can easily go into websites to get share price information, company news and financials, which makes direct offshore investing easy. Offshore newspapers, magazines and sharebrokers are all on-line – it is as easy to get the news on-line from New York as it is from Auckland. (In fact, it's easier from New York because the websites are better.)

In spite of the amount of information available from offshore, it is still quite hard to get a feel for what is happening and how things work. If you are planning to invest offshore directly yourself, take things slowly. Watch the markets and your target companies for a while and, when you feel ready to move, invest in small amounts. Don't be in any hurry to put a major proportion of your available funds offshore – there is no hurry. If waiting means that you miss out on something, don't worry – there will be more good investments coming along, there always are.

There are hundreds, maybe thousands, of good Internet sites that you can use to get offshore information. Indeed, there are now books published which give the names and addresses of Internet sites that would be of interest to investors (e.g. *The Internet for Investing and Personal Finance*, Martin Roth, Wright Books, Australia).

The sites that I use mostly are:

www.bloomberg.com

This gives real-time share prices and indices as well as market commentaries, company financials, research and news along with other money information (e.g. on mortgages). It also checks through to Bloomberg's UK site.

www.fool.com

This comes from Motley Fool and has a wealth of financial and market information.

www.afr.co.au

This is the *Australian Financial Review*'s site and has all the business, financial and investment news and information that you could want. Some of the portfolio management and company information is only available on subscription.

www.market-eye.co.uk

Again, everything you could want, especially if you subscribe.

INFORMATION OVERLOAD

These days, getting lots of information and data is not really a problem. There is plenty available from a range of sources. The difficulty is often putting that information into a form that is usable and readily accessible. This has become a lot easier with computers and on-line information. It is easier to store information in a computer and much easier to access it from there than in boxes of cuttings and broker reports (and much easier than a metre-high pile of *National Business Reviews*).

The most useful information is that which affects the businesses you are interested in. The decisions on what is useful and what to keep really hinge on whether a piece of information will actually affect the business or not. It is useful to imagine that you own the business (as in fact you do – well, a little bit of it). If you owned all of the company, what would be the things that would make its prospects better or worse? If you were managing it, what things would make your job harder or easier? This sense of ownership is crucial in deciding what is important and what is not. Believing and feeling that you own a business helps relieve information overload. Shares are not a commodity to be traded – they represent ownership of a little bit of a business. It is the prospects for that business that you need information on, not all the other noise of the markets. Take ownership, pretend that you are running the business and then decide what is important from that perspective.

NETWORKS

Share investing can be a solitary activity. It is quite possible to invest on the sharemarket without ever talking to anyone – and many people do. However, it is a good idea to have some contacts, people who you can talk to about what you are doing, what they are doing and for finding out what is going on. Having a share network is a good idea.

Those who use full-service brokers will already have someone that they can talk to. However, meeting other people with an interest in shares may not be easy. You may have friends or family or even workmates who you can talk to and whose opinions you respect. Beyond those people, you should attend investment seminars and go to the annual general meetings of companies that you are interested in. Both these functions will be full of people who are share investors.

You should also join the New Zealand Shareholders' Association (**www.nzshareholders.co.nz**). This is a fairly new group but has

The more people that you talk to and listen to, the better you will understand the thoughts and feelings of the market.

already made an impact with its activism and advocacy on behalf of small shareholders. The association has a website and puts out a newsletter, and in some centres holds meetings. It is well worth supporting by being a member, partly because it is doing a very good job, but also for increasing the people you know who are share investors.

A market is simply a collection of people, each with a view on whether it is a good idea to buy or to sell. The more people that you talk to and listen to, the better you will understand the thoughts and feelings of the market.

WAY SIX

Gear for super-profits

Gearing is the quickest way to beat the market. It can also be a speedy way to get disqualified and thrown out of the race. It depends entirely on how you go about it and what you do. Your judgement geared up with borrowings can give you quick riches or send you straight to the doss-house. Gearing ups the ante, increases the stakes.

Smart investors often use gearing. They use it because they back themselves. They back their knowledge, their skills and their judgement. They know that if they get it right (and they do expect to get it right), gearing will put them way ahead of the pack. In fact, most serious investors, and nearly all who are winners, use gearing in some form or other. However, they do not necessarily use the old ways of simply borrowing from a bank or finance company on the security of the share scrip. Instead, they look to new means to get the same effect with things like derivatives, futures, warrants and options. Some of these are so good they can be done in such a way as to protect your capital and limit your downside risk.

> **Gearing is the quickest way to beat the market.**

Gearing by itself will let you beat the market. You don't have to do any clever stock picking or trading, borrowing to buy shares will put you ahead. Even if you simply borrowed to buy the index, an average performance, the borrowings that you take on will increase the returns and so put you ahead. The one big proviso with this is, of course, that the market rises – if it doesn't, you have trouble. However, we know that over long periods of time the markets have always risen and it's reasonable to suppose that in spite of the ups and downs it will continue to do so. Gearing, even in its simplest form, let alone use of some of the more sophisticated techniques, will help you be better than average.

PRINCIPLES OF GEARING

Like the gears in a car, investment gearing allows you to go faster without having to speed up the motor. The higher the gear you choose, the faster that you will go (and the bigger the crash if something goes wrong). The idea of borrowing to buy investments is to allow you to own more of the investment than would otherwise be the case and so you get the upside of a greater share portfolio. This works well – provided that you make the right investment decisions. You may have to pay interest on your borrowings (sometimes your dividends will cover the interest payments), but over long periods of time the interest will be well compensated for by the capital gains.

Gearing (it's sometimes called leverage) lets you buy more of an asset than you could otherwise afford. You use the money that you have, borrow some more and so buy a bigger number of shares.

For example, say you have $20,000. There are two options:

1. You buy $20,000 of shares. These go up in one year by 20% and so now you have a holding worth $24,000 – a capital profit of $4000. In addition to that, you would have dividends of say $1000 (a 5% dividend yield), which would be taxed leaving you with approximately $600.

   You have a total profit of $4600.

2. You use your $20,000 as a deposit and borrow another $30,000. Now you have a total portfolio of $50,000. If that goes up by 20%, you have capital profits of $10,000. In addition you would have $2500 of dividends. However, you would have

to pay interest, which at 10% p.a. would cost $3000 on your $30,000. That would be paid for out of dividends, leaving you with a cash loss of $500.

However, your overall profit there is $9500.

	UNGEARED INVESTOR Option 1	GEARED INVESTOR Option 2
Shares purchased	$20,000	$50,000
New value (20%)	$24,000	$60,000
Capital profit	$4000	$10,000
Dividends	$1000	$2500
Borrowing costs	–	$3000
Tax	$400	nil
Profit on dividends	$600	($500)
Total profit	$2600	$9500

In fact, the situation for the geared investor is somewhat better than this. The loss that the borrowing investor has made ($500 in this case) would be deductible against other income, giving a tax benefit. Borrowings to buy investments (whether shares or property) are tax deductible. By borrowing, you give up some taxable income (dividends) but increase your non-taxable capital gains. Gearing up can be very tax efficient in a country like New Zealand where there is no capital gains tax – effectively you convert taxable income in the form of dividends to non-taxable capital gains. It is quite common for property investors to make a tax loss on their borrowed investments – i.e. for borrowing costs to exceed cash income. This is called negative gearing – it works just as well for share investments as it does for property investors.

Of course, gearing creates greater risks. If the shares in the above example had fallen by 20% in value, the loss for the ungeared investor would be $4000, but the investor who had borrowed would have lost half of the original capital used – i.e. $10,000.

	UNGEARED INVESTOR Option 1	GEARED INVESTOR Option 2
Shares purchased	$20,000	$50,000
New value (–20%)	$16,000	$40,000
Loss	$4000	$10,000

It may well be worse for the geared investor. That investor still has to pay interest and so is continuing to fund the difference between dividends and borrowings ($500) out of other resources. And of course if dividends are reduced or interest rates rise, the geared investor could be in real trouble.

There would be little or no problem with gearing if the arrangement was always made for long periods of time. If you take just about any 10-year period, the returns from shares (both dividends and capital growth) would almost always be greater than the cost of borrowings. The trouble with a lot of gearing to buy shares is that it is often for short periods. Whether it is a margin trading facility, a warrant or even a bank loan, you need to get your timing right. A down period straight after you have purchased which ends up lasting a year or two can be a disaster.

There is a fair bit of rubbish talked about gearing up to buy investments. Some will say that property is the best investment to borrow for because banks like lending on property and it is therefore easy. The first of these assertions is true – banks do like lending on property. They may also lend on the security of shares but will not lend as much and the interest rate will be higher. The second is not true – it is in fact much easier to gear up to buy shares than it is to gear up on property. In fact, you can gear up to buy shares without ever going near a bank or a banker (something which quite a few people would consider to be attractive!). Instead of approaching a bank with a proposal and going through the time-consuming carry-on and expense of getting approval and securing the mortgage, you can simply

> **The real trouble with gearing for shares is the volatility of the market.**

buy warrants or options or instalment receipts, or establish a margin trading facility. All of these provide gearing very easily and simply.

The real trouble with gearing for shares is the volatility of the market. Property investors routinely borrow to buy their investments and yet in the long term, over most periods of time, the returns from shares are usually better than from property. But the volatility of the stockmarket creates a lot of noise which so often tends to panic share investors. The value of your holding is there to see every day, even every minute, and it is so easy to sell out of shares. This causes share investors to think and act in the short term.

YOUR OWN LITTLE SUPER FUND

If you could be sure of holding your nerve and keeping your share portfolio for a long period of time (10 or, even better, 20 years), owning a geared portfolio would work out just as well for share investors as it would for property investors, probably better. Property investors often buy a property as their own little superannuation fund; share investors could do the same.

For example, the 1990s were not the best times for the New Zealand market. If you had bought $10,000 of shares in January 1990, by January 2000 you would have had a portfolio valued at $13,300. This is not a great return (about 3% after tax) although you would also have had dividends, meaning your gross return would probably be better than holding cash in the bank.

However, if you had geared this portfolio by borrowing $20,000, the value of your equity would be:

	WITHOUT GEARING	WITH GEARING
Shares purchased 1.1.90	$10,000	$30,000
Value 1.1.2000	$13,300	$39,900
Less borrowings	–	($20,000)
Profit	$3300	$9900

Note that the geared investor has almost double the original capital. Even at a time of relative non-performance, in a poor market and without any stock picking, the investor has a return of around 7% p.a. tax paid. That compares reasonably well with other investments, even when investing in one of the worst decades on record.

Note that this scenario assumes a number of things:

1. Dividends would at least cover the cost of borrowing.

2. You remain disciplined and focused and do not lose your nerve. It's not easy to keep on paying interest for months or years while your investments fail to perform or head downwards. Conversely, you may become very tempted to take your profit at some point when the market is strong.

The strategy of buying a substantial block of shares by borrowing is a reasonably conservative one (certainly no more risky than buying a second house), provided you:

- diversify the holdings.
- hold long term – 10–20 years.
- are disciplined.
- time the purchase reasonably (i.e. not while shares are very high – the year 2000 or 2008 would not have been a good time to borrow for shares).
- have a little luck (no disastrous economic recession).

I doubt that the risks involved in doing this are any greater than gearing up to buy a rental property, something which tens of thousands of New Zealanders have done quite happily and with little thought over the last few years. In fact, given the diversification of the investments, it could be argued that it is less risky. I also doubt that it would be much less profitable.

It is therefore somewhat surprising that more people do not do it!

The approach described above, where you borrow to buy a basket of shares which approximates the index, might beat the market but is by no means the most sophisticated, the least risky, nor the best way to go about gearing into sharemarket investments. There are other ways and other products which are easier, better and carry less risk while retaining no less upside potential. Some of these require no more than signing a piece of paper and handing over your money – and they have no recourse back on you if things go wrong. Some even give a capital guarantee!

INSTALMENT WARRANTS

These are based on a portfolio of blue chip shares and put into practice the principle of buying a good investment portfolio, gearing it up and holding it long term. The investor puts up a deposit, usually around 50%, and the balance is provided by way of a loan from the promoter/bank. This loan is a non-recourse one, i.e. during the period of ownership the bank will not ask for principal repayments and, if the shares have performed very badly at the end of the period and are worth less than the borrowings, you will not have to make up that deficit. The dividends from the shares will go towards paying interest. If there is a deficit you will have to make that up, but if there's anything left it will repay principal.

Instalment warrants are usually held for some years – perhaps as long as 10 years. At the end of that period, any outstanding principal is repaid and you exercise your warrant and take delivery of your portfolio of shares. In fact, in a practical sense, this whole final set of transactions will happen at the same time: the shares will be sold, outstanding principal repaid and you will receive a cheque for the balance. Obviously the

> There have been very few times over the history of the sharemarket when a parcel of good quality shares has not risen in value over a 10-year period.

size of that cheque will depend entirely on how well the portfolio of shares has done over the years.

Instalment warrants are offered in New Zealand by Macquarie Bank and Challenger Equities. You can choose which shares you want to invest in from their list of approved companies in Australia and New Zealand. Instalment warrants represent a very good way to gear into a share portfolio with relatively little risk. There have been very few times over the history of the sharemarket when a parcel of good quality shares has not risen in value over a 10-year period. Certainly if you had purchased an instalment warrant at the height of the market in 2000 you would still have lost out 10 years later, but that is an exception. The non-recourse loan and the long period of time that endowment warrants are for make them a very good option for passive investors.

MARGIN TRADING

This has been given the blame for major run-ups of shares in the 1920s and in the 1980s, and at the same time for the crashes that have followed. Margin trading is perhaps the classic way to borrow to buy shares.

Margin trading is usually done through sharebrokers or through a specialist firm or finance company. These proliferate during bull runs as brokerage and finance companies look to profit by lending money at a good interest rate (usually about 3–4% over bank bills). This is not an especially high interest rate, only one or two percentage points over what you would pay for your house mortgage.

Generally, the lender will have the shares registered in its own name – it holds the shares as security for your borrowings. Nevertheless, you are responsible for the purchase and, of course, for the repayment of the amount that you have borrowed to buy them.

Most providers of margin facilities ask few questions about you or your financial standing. The shares themselves are regarded as good enough security. This is not necessarily because the lender regards the shares that you have purchased as first-rate and never likely to fall in value. Rather it is because of the way the lender requires you to keep up your margin (or deposit) and because of the ruthless way that it will sell the shares if there is any likelihood of a loss.

YOUR MARGIN

When you buy shares through a margin trading facility, you have to put up a deposit. This deposit may be 20% to 50% of the total value of shares that you are buying. The deposit is called a 'margin'. You have to maintain your margin at all times when the shares that you have bought fall in value. The margin is in fact your lender's margin for safety. The size of the deposit, whether it is 25% or 50% of the value of the shares, depends on the type of shares that you are buying. Blue chip shares, those of bigger companies and those which have a busy market with lots of trades, may require a margin of only 25%. Smaller companies whose shares are less frequently traded may require a margin of 50% – it is harder for a lender to sell out of these quickly if the need arises.

The lender will want to see the margin maintained at all times. If the shares fall in value, the lender will phone and require you to deposit cash immediately to restore the margin to the agreed level (whether that is 25% or 50%). This is the dreaded 'margin call'. If you do not meet the margin call immediately by putting up more cash, the lender can and will immediately sell the shares. Because of the volatility of the sharemarket and because it can move very quickly, the margin lender will sell straight away, usually within 48 hours of the margin call (assuming you haven't topped up the margin with cash).

On the other hand, if the shares rise in value your margin will have increased – you will have more of your equity in the deal both in percentage and dollar terms. This will mean that if you want to, you can use the greater equity you have through the increased value of your shares to borrow more money. In effect you are using the unrealised profit as equity for another lot of borrowings to buy more shares. There are people who do this whenever they can, continually using the growth in value of their shares to borrow more money and so hold a bigger and bigger portfolio.

Margin traders must get their timing right. It is common enough for shares to fall in value after they are bought, only to move back up later. While this is not a problem for most sharemarket investors, it can be very difficult and painful for those buying shares on a margin.

For example, in January 2008 you decide to purchase ABC at 200c. The deal looks like this:

Date:	January 2008
Shares purchased:	6000 ABC at 200¢
Total purchase price:	$12,000
Financing:	$9000 at 9.5%
Margin:	$3000 (25%)
Date:	February 2008
Shares fall to 166c	
Value of holding is now $10,000	
Margin is now only $1000 (10%)	
Call from lender – please deposit $1,500 to bring margin to $2,500 (25% of $10,000 value)	
Date:	March 2010
Shares fall to 100c	
Value of holding is now $6000	
Margin has gone	
Another margin call for $3000	
Time to sell!	
Total loss is $6000	

This sort of thing happens often enough. Most experienced margin traders might have cut their losses earlier – they may have picked the downward trend early and sold out. However, they just might have held on longer, to their cost: ABC might have gone to 90c before it bottomed out.

However, to balance things up, here is a successful deal, the sort of thing that margin traders live for. It concerns Fletcher Building Ltd, purchased in March 2001 at 225c.

Date:	March 2001
Shares purchased:	10,000 Fletcher Building at 225¢
Total purchase price:	$22,500
Financing:	$15,750 at 9.5%
Margin:	$6750 (30%)

The shares do well, climbing in value with barely a pause.

Date:	February 2002
Shares rise to 300¢	
Value of holding is now $30,000	
Profit (on deposit of $6750) is $7500	

Decide to hold on a bit yet!

Date:	October 2002
Shares go to 330c	
Value of holding is now $33,000	

Decide to sell.

Profit is	$10,500
Plus dividend received	$1800
	$12,300
Less interest cost	($2400)
Net profit	$9900

This profit was on a cash input of $6,750 and made in such a short time. That's why margin traders are margin traders!

Timing is critical to successful margins trading. If you can, you want to buy at times which have limited downside. Such times are:

- During rights trading. When there is a cash issue, many shareholders sell some of their rights, weakening the share price. This is often a good time to buy.

- Before annual meetings, a time when there is often an upward movement in share price.
- Before the announcement of a bonus issue – some companies do this nearly every year, when they announce their financial result.

Margin trading has been responsible for significant falls in the market. Large numbers of people owning shares on borrowed money causes what might have been a market slump to turn into a full-scale rout. If the market starts to fall a little, many people do not have the cash to meet their margin call and have to sell at a loss. They are selling into a market which is already weak – the slump becomes a panic as people scramble to get out. This becomes a vicious circle which feeds on itself. Smaller companies where there is not a big busy market can be especially difficult to offload as there may not be buyers at any price. This can put the share price of such companies into a free fall.

Although margin trading is risky, the rewards can be great. If you are going to margin trade, you need to be very clear-headed – always act from the head, never the heart. There are some basic rules for margin traders:

1. Time your purchases as well as you can (much easier said than done).
2. Be sufficiently cashed up to meet a margin call, or be prepared to sell at a loss.
3. Buy into larger companies whose shares are frequently traded (you may need to be able to get out quickly).

You should also be sure that you can meet the monthly interest payments!

WARRANTS

Warrants are based on individual shares. They give you the right (but not the obligation) to purchase a share at some point in the future for a particular price (called the 'exercise price'). Warrants are usually promoted by a merchant bank and sold to the public then listed on the sharemarket.

The key to warrants is that once you own them you do not have any obligation to buy the head shares on which the warrant is based. If the head shares have fallen in value, you can simply ignore the warrant, recognising that it is now valueless. If you own a warrant and that gives you the right to buy a share for 500c but the share has fallen to 350c, you do not have to go ahead and pay 500c for something which is now only worth 350c. The amount of your loss is limited to what you paid on the market for the warrant.

This gives gearing with very low risk. Because you have no obligation to buy the share you can only lose what you have paid for your warrant. You are able to take control of a large block of shares with only limited downside risk.

Warrants have five key components:

1. The company on which the warrant is based (e.g. Telecom or Contact Energy).
2. The premium that you pay. This initially goes to the bank that floated the warrant, but once the warrant is floated and trades on the market that is effectively the price of it. Once listed, the warrant will trade at a value set by the market, generally in line with the value of the head share.
3. The date at which the warrant is to be exercised. This is the time at which you can purchase the head share. The exercise date is often around two years from when the warrant was first floated, making it a fairly short-term play.
4. The price that you must pay to convert your warrant to the share. This is called the strike or exercise price.
5. The conversion terms. Sometimes you will need two or three warrants for each share, although some warrants convert at 1:1.

For example, you may purchase a Telecom warrant for 50c, giving you the right to purchase a Telecom share for 300c in March 2013. At the time, Telecom may be trading at 200c. There is something of a gamble in this: if the Telecom share price rises to say, 400c, you can exercise your warrant at 300c and with a total cost of 350c (warrant price of 50c plus 300c for the share) you have made a good profit. However, if the Telecom share price does not rise, you have a valueless warrant which you end up throwing in the rubbish bin.

The real gamble here is time: Telecom one day may well reach 300c. The question is whether it will reach 300c by the exercise date, i.e. March 2013.

Warrants are traded on the New Zealand Stock Exchange. The valuation of them can be very complex as investors need to take account of not just the value of a Telecom share and the prospects for Telecom's business but also the time value of money. After all, you have paid 50c to take control of a much larger asset (a good gearing effect) – you have not had to outlay the whole price of the share. You do not have to pay interest on the money you have 'borrowed'; neither do you get dividends because you do not own the shares. You only have the right to buy them at some point in the future.

Broadly, the price of warrants will go up and down as the head share moves. The percentage changes will be great – if Telecom moves up 50c, the warrant will also go up by around the same amount. If Telecom shares go up from 300c to 350c, that is an increase of 17%. However, if your warrant goes from 50c to 100c that is an increase of 100%. This is the value of the gearing effect.

However, many warrants over recent years have not finished 'in the money' – that is, they have ended their lives thrown in the rubbish bin, valueless. The sharemarket and the individual shares on which warrants are based have simply not performed well enough. While this is obviously not desirable, it may not be quite the disaster for someone who has purchased warrants as might be imagined. This is provided that the warrant holder has not overextended his purchase and only bought as many warrants as he would have purchased shares.

For example, the investor may have been going to buy 5000 Telecom shares at 200c for a total price of $10,000. Had he done this and the Telecom share price went sideways and basically stayed at 200c after three years, he would have the dividends but no capital profit. Instead, had he bought 5000 warrants at 50c, he would have outlayed $2500 and lost all of that. However, he would have had the balance of his funds, $7500, sitting in the bank getting interest. If it got 5% interest for three years it would have grown by around $375. This makes up part of the capital loss of $2500.

There are two important factors that the warrant holder has covered:

1. Had the share collapsed in value, the warrant holder's loss was always limited to $2500. The potential loss for the investor who purchased the shares directly was $10,000 – he could conceivably have lost the lot.

2. Had the share price gone up strongly the warrant holder's profit would be just as great as (or greater than) the direct shareholder.

It is only when the shares mess in the middle that the warrant purchaser may be a little worse off. That seems to me to be a small enough price to pay for covering the downside while still being able to enjoy the upside.

It is quite feasible and reasonable to buy warrants instead of shares as a long-term investment. If you were going to buy 5,000 Telecom shares at 200c (a total of $10,000), you might instead outlay only $2500, buying 5000 Telecom warrants at 50c. You can hold the other $7500 in the bank. The key thing is to make sure that on the exercise date, when the warrant has expired, you purchase either new warrants or shares. It would

> **It is quite feasible to buy warrants instead of shares as a long-term investment.**

be galling indeed for the shares to have languished for three years (or even gone down in value) only for them to go up rapidly just after the warrant had expired. Such a possibility needs to be covered – if this is a long-term investment, you need some sort of exposure to the company at all times.

I think warrants are often an excellent alternative to buying shares. The only trouble with them is that there are very few listed on the New Zealand sharemarket at present. This is because New Zealand shares have not done well, reducing the attractiveness of them both for investors and the banks that organise and release them. However, other markets (Australia, USA, UK, etc) have thousands of them – most significant companies will have warrants issued. When the New Zealand market starts to perform better, there will again be more warrants issued and you should at the very least consider them instead of buying ordinary shares.

OPTIONS – PUT AND CALL

Call options are the same in most respects as warrants. Again, they give the right to buy a share without any obligation, and they trade on the market. These tradeable options should not be confused with staff options, which are provided as a performance incentive to managers of a company (often far too generously).

Put options are the opposite of call options and warrants. They give you the right to *sell* a share at a particular price on a particular date. Put options are for people who believe a share might fall in value – if you have the right to 'put' a share to someone at say 300c and the share has fallen to 200c, you can buy shares at 200c on the exercise date to deliver to the other party and take a profit of 100c on the transaction. In fact, in a practical sense you do not have to buy the share at 200c and deliver it to the buyer – the profit is reflected in the price of the option as it trades on the market. People use put options for speculative purposes and also to hedge, if they are holding particular shares and fear a fall in value.

INTELLIGENT GEARING

Intelligent gearing is a great way to beat the market. Good gearing will almost certainly include warrants (including endowment warrants). Short-term trading of warrants and margin trading are fraught with difficulty and are probably only for the most experienced investors and traders. But careful gearing for the long haul will let many investors beat the market.

WAY SEVEN

Plan, plan, plan

In 1978 I had some spare cash. I had heard of this thing called a sharemarket and decided to have a go. I made an appointment to see a broker and sat down in his office after the market had closed for the day.

'*What are your aims?*' he asked. '*Long term, short term? What sort of things are you looking for?*'

'*Well, ummmmm . . .*' I hesitated.

'*Just something that'll make you some money,*' he said, interrupting my indecision which clearly displayed my ignorance.

We talked about a few things and I left having ordered about $3000 worth of shares (some Smith City and Winstone, I think), about which I knew virtually nothing.

And so for some years I stumbled and bumbled through the market, making a bit of money but only because you had to be fairly stupid (or seriously unlucky) not to do well in those days. Certainly I had no plan and no strategy and did no analysis. I followed my broker's recommendations without any clear idea of what I was doing. When I did as I was told and bought something, I didn't know whether I had bought it as a long-term hold or as a short-term trade. Thus I would sell because something had gone up 20% (not knowing that it was predicted to keep rising for years) or hold on to something which would rise for a bit and then fall (not knowing that it was a special situation to be in and out of quickly).

I didn't know whether I was a trader or investor. I would find that I had to sell because I needed the money for something, and in selling take a loss because what I had bought was a slow but steady performer. The brokers must have done well out of me as I thrashed around, continually turning over shares, always looking for something that would 'make me a bit of money'. I was successful enough but only because the markets were good – if I only knew then what I know now!

People often ask me what is the best investment; where should they put their money? What they are looking for is someone to tell them to dive into certain types of property, or offer tips on shares. But investment is not like that. Investment is about planning in terms of you as an individual, and about matching yourself to investments to get a good fit. You cannot give good investment advice without knowing the individual concerned – the investor's personality, family circumstances and financial position. You can't invest properly by stumbling off into the markets looking for things that 'will make you a bit of money'.

KEEP IT SMALL, KEEP IT SIMPLE

Having shown that I am a great fan of planning, some readers may be relieved to know that I am no supporter of plans that run to pages and pages.

A plan needs to be a working document, something that you use all the time. The plan needs to drive your daily behaviour; it needs to dictate what you do. As such, you should be able to carry it around in your head. That is not to say that it should not be written down – it should! But if you are going to have a plan and, more particularly if you are going to use the plan, you do not want to have to dive off into the bottom drawer of your desk to retrieve then read some 15-page document every time you are going to do something.

> **A plan needs to be a working document, something that you use all the time.**

A beautifully written and presented 15-page plan might look nice, and you might carry out the things that are in it when it is first written. But investment decisions are ongoing – you can't just do a plan, implement it then forget it. The plan has to keep you on your track over the coming weeks, months and years.

EASY DECISION-MAKING

A good plan makes decision-making easy. That is really the point of a plan and it works as long as it is in a form to dictate what you do. A simple plan is quick and easy to refer to and means that it is easy to decide what to do when new investment opportunities arise. For example, if your plan says that you should have 10% of your share portfolio in short-term (and risky) trading stocks and you actually have 12% in that sort of thing, it should be a complete no-brainer to say 'no!' when there is an IPO in some wild idea to cure HIV/AIDS.

That is why you have a plan. You have decided what you are going to do at a quiet time, a time when you can think and when you are not emotionally involved. Your decisions have been made with your head, in the absence of any feelings of fear or greed. You would need to be fairly brave to override such planning. Planning lets you *think* rather than *feel.*

Having a plan in a form that is not big and complicated means that the important things are noted down and in the front of your mind. It is the key goals and strategies that are important, not the detail. A plan for shares should be able to go on one sheet of paper, two at the most. That way you will be able to use it – on a daily basis. Your plan will be central to everything that you do, the reference point for all of your decisions.

So, how do you get such a paragon of a plan? The answer to that is:

Purpose
Ends
Strategies
Targets

PEST is the best model that I know for planning for a business. And it works just as well for investment planning. However, before I look at PEST in detail and show some sample share plans, you need to think about *yourself* as an investor.

You cannot set objectives and goals if you do not know yourself. This is not navel-gazing contemplation, it is a consideration of where you are (financially) and the type of person that you are as an investor (your financial personality). Investment planning is like taking a trip: a map is of no use if you do not know where you are starting from. You cannot hope to plan a journey if you cannot pinpoint your position on a map.

You cannot set objectives and goals if you do not know yourself.

WHO ARE YOU?

Your money in general and your investments in particular should make a happy fit with your situation and your personality. Investing and having money are not an end in themselves – they are a means to a better life. If your finances do not fit neatly with who you are the result will be unhappy frustration.

Just as important in a book aimed to help you 'beat the market', if you do not find an investment style that suits you, you will not achieve your goals. Remember that with shares there is a wide spectrum that gives you a choice as to how to make money on the market – everyone, from the speculating day traders to those who buy shares, puts them in the bottom drawer and forgets them. Where you place yourself on that spectrum requires some thought, so that you act and operate in the market in the way that suits you best.

This section is not designed to give a definitive investment personality type where each person scores a number. Rather its intention is to flush out some of the issues which will dictate how you decide to invest on the market and how you might split your portfolio. Remember that you do not need to operate on the market in just one mode: you can use part of your available funds for long-term investing and hold some back for trading. If you think about the issues below you should be able to proportion your funds appropriately.

Some of the issues are of a technical, black-or-white nature – your tax position, age, financial position, etc. Others are of a less defined nature – your boredom threshold, general personality, appetite for risk. It is sometimes a good idea (and perhaps more fun) to get someone to work through these items with you. This could be a spouse or partner who knows you well and can act as a check for you. It is important that this suitability process is done honestly – the more accurate it is the better. Even if you do not like the idea of having a low boredom threshold, if that is what you are like you may as well know about it so that you can act accordingly.

The eight areas that you need to think about are:

1. **Time frame for investing.** Getting this wrong is the second greatest cause of people losing money on the sharemarket (the greatest cause is 'hot' tips from a family member). Getting the time frame right means thinking about when you are going to need your money back. Most share investing should be for at least three years. That is roughly an economic cycle – we are unlikely to have many down times or recessions that last for that long. At some time within three years there are likely to be good economic or business periods that should mean your investments do well. However, three years is an absolute minimum: ideally you will commit to a 10-year time frame. There have been a few times in history when you would have lost money owning shares for that long: for example, if you had bought US shares in 2000, you would still not have got your money back in 2010. But the chances of this are fairly slim and you would have to have bought into a bubble at the very top.

> **Getting the time frame right means thinking about when you are going to need your money back.**

Getting this time frame wrong and having to sell at a point which is not of your choosing can be a disaster. Sometimes you might have to break your time frame unexpectedly. You could get struck by one of the three Ds – death, divorce or other disaster. There's not much you can do about this – you simply have to sell up and if the time is not right take the loss, if there's one there, on the chin.

However, sometimes people break their time frame simply because they have planned badly (or not planned at all). This sees people selling up to pay their tax or to add another bedroom on the house – the sale of shares at such times is almost always at a loss.

Think very carefully about how long you are investing for and try to plan for every eventuality. You will never get this perfectly correct but that shouldn't stop you from trying. If you are likely to need your money inside of five years, you should really go about things as a trader rather than an investor and adopt the rules for trading accordingly, or leave your money in the bank.

2. **Skill level.** This is one of those subjective personal attributes which needs to be assessed honestly. Fortunately, if you do come out low on the scale in terms of your investment/ finance/ business skills, it is something that you can correct.

   If you do not have great skills you should start slowly with the bulk of your money in either managed funds (perhaps an index tracker) or in a few solid companies and only gradually put significant funds into less well-known companies. Use a full-service sharebroker and utilise their research and advice. Read all you can, listen to all you can, learn all you can. However, there is no substitute for getting into the market and doing it. You will make mistakes – just be sure that you are not using a lot of money and that you learn from those mistakes.

3. **Your time.** Choose the way in which you are going to invest on the sharemarket according to the amount of time you are prepared

to commit to your investing. People who are not prepared to devote time to investing should look for long-term holdings or even invest through managed funds. More active investment and trading requires time. If you already have a spouse and four children, two jobs, are on the City Council, and are in training for a marathon, setting up an active share trading operation would be a really bad idea.

People at each end of the financial spectrum can afford to take some risks – those in the middle cannot.

4. **Financial position.** People at each end of the financial spectrum can afford to take some risks – those in the middle cannot. Those with no (or only very little) money can take risks because they have little to lose; those with a lot of assets can also take some risks because it does not matter if they lose a bit. However, those in the middle, those who have some assets but who are still financially vulnerable, cannot take risks. Age may come into this – older people often being more risk averse because they will have less time to recover financial mistakes. These people should largely eschew trading and should not borrow to invest but rather stay with good long-term solid shares.

5. **Tax position.** Trading and investing are treated differently for tax purposes (see Chapter Four). If you have a large amount of taxable income from your job or business already, you may not want to add to it by trading. This is especially so if some profitable trading would put you into a higher tax bracket. If you are already paying quite a lot of tax you should tend towards sharemarket activities that are tax efficient. This may mean investing long term so that the capital profits are not taxable; it may mean investing in companies where most of the profits are retained by the company for growth instead of paid out as taxable dividends; or

Make an honest assessment of the amount of risk with which you are comfortable.

it may mean using gearing techniques to increase non-taxable capital growth at the expense of taxable income.

6. **Risk.** Investment risk needs to be thought about in two ways. First, as it relates to your financial position (see above). Second, it should be considered as a personality matter. If you worry about money, even lose sleep over it, you are better to have a widely diversified holding of solid shares. If you are risk averse, not only will more risky investments make you unhappy, it is likely that the emotion will cloud your judgement and have you making panic decisions which are not necessarily in your best interests. Make an honest assessment of the amount of risk with which you are comfortable.

7. **Boredom threshold.** Some people are just not suited to having all of their money tied up in long-term investments, ones that grow steadily but not spectacularly and where little happens month by month. If you fit into that category, you may as well admit it and make sure that part of your money is in shorter-term trades. The alternative is that you will end up selling those long-term boring investments because you lack the patience. (I know someone who has gone into a super fund three times. Each time he has got bored with it within five years and has cashed it up, always at a considerable loss.)

   The lower your boredom threshold, the more money you should allocate to trading (and the more you should concentrate on getting your trading right). There are people who become almost addicted to buying shares – they get some sort of buzz from placing buy orders and seeing those shares added to their portfolio. This might be all right if you have unlimited funds with which to keep on buying – anyone else (which is just about everyone) should recognise their 'buy problem' and learn either to curtail their buying or to sell a bit. A low boredom threshold is not really something which can be 'fixed'. You can only recognise it and arrange your portfolio so that you don't get bored. You will know at a conscious level that most of your profits will come from buying into good businesses and holding them long term – but you may need a bit of excitement. Having said that, a warning: in my experience, the most exciting investments are those that make money!

8. **Personality.** This is the least easily defined area. People have personalities which will push them one way or another with their investments. Right from the start, some will want to beat the market while others will be quite satisfied with a good enough or average performance.

Self-assessment in terms of personality is not easy. However, before you become engrossed in share investment it is worth thinking about what you are like and what you are suited to under four headings:

- **People skills.** Share investment can be a lonely activity. My guess is that the top investors are quite introverted, happy to shut themselves off from other people while they do some analysis, relaxed with their own company. Preferring to interact with people does not of course preclude successful share investment, but it does mean that you may need to train yourself to close the office door while you concentrate on some analysis even though that is not what you really want to do.
- **Detail.** Looking at the big picture is important because you need to know what is going on in the world, what is driving trends and where money is being made. However, ultimately the devil of good share analysis is in the detail. You must knuckle down to detail or be prepared to rely on someone else's analysis (e.g. your broker or a tip sheet). For those who don't like fine detail, that's not a very attractive message – but that's how it is.
- **Feelings.** When it comes to investment, 'feel' is a four-letter word. Top investors think and then act – they do not rely on their feelings. If your preference is to act on feelings, you must train yourself to suppress emotion (when it comes to invest-

ment!). As shown earlier in Way One: Know the markets, most people in the market decide to buy or sell on the basis of fear or greed (which are emotions). To beat them, you *need to think*.

> To beat the market you do need to be decisive.

- **Decision-making.** Some people make good, firm decisions quickly while others like to keep their options open as they dither and mess around. In investment, this dithering can see people end up buying a few shares in just about everything. To beat the market you do need to be decisive – analyse and then put your money into just a few companies, backing yourself to be right. Fortune favours the brave – it does not favour dithering.

All of these things will dictate how you will buy or sell shares: your sharemarket style. Everyone needs to own shares but there are many different ways of doing so. Thinking about all of these things will help you decide about:

- How much you want to beat the market by.
- The proportion of your portfolio in investing or trading.
- The amount of gearing (borrowing) you may do.
- The degree of diversification.
- Whether you use a full-service broker or rely on your own advice.
- The amount you might have in managed funds.
- The skills you need to develop.

None of the eight factors that you need to think about stands alone, none is decisive by itself. Rather, they make up an amalgam all together. For some people one or two (or three or four) factors may be far more important than the others, pushing them off in one direction or another. It is impossible to give points to each so that you come up with a score on a particular item. Instead, you have to weigh each factor in terms of your own situation and position, and apply some common sense. This is not something which can be done by numbers.

Nevertheless, it is important that it is done. Beating the market is hard enough without first developing a strategy. That strategy can only come after looking at your current position, knowing where you are and who you are. To do anything else is to thrash around in hope.

PEST

So – how then do you make a plan that you live, breathe and invest with, which drives your every financial thought? The answer is with a good format. A good format keeps you to a particular route, a route which has the ultimate direction in mind at all times but has regular markers to keep you on the path.

The formula that I have already noted has four components:

Purpose
Ends
Strategies
Targets

PEST is a cascading format whereby what is decided in each of the components flows from the preceding one. A decision in one area dictates what will be done in the next area. For example, a particular purpose dictates the ends; certain stated ends will dictate strategy, which in turn leads to targets.

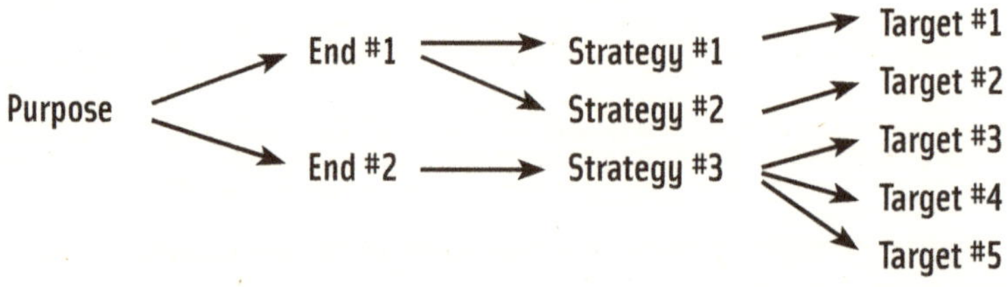

To know your desired ends (or goals) you must be mindful of your purpose; to know what strategies you will employ you must think about your ends; and before you can consider what targets (or individual companies) to go for, you must think about your strategies. Each flows from one to the next – therefore all are related. The result is an integrated plan – and one that you should be able to fit onto one piece of paper!

The key to this plan is that each of the parts fits together with the others. Each can only be settled after regard to the preceding one, forcing you to always set your plan with reference to your main purpose and your ends. I find it a very easy plan to use.

It may not look as impressive or as valuable as its 15-page equivalent – but because you can actually use it, it is!

P IS FOR PURPOSE

This should be the easiest part of the planning process. It is simply answering the question: Why are you investing in shares in the first place? Although perhaps easy to answer, it is very important to do. To be successful with shares, you should have a clearly defined purpose, know exactly what it is that you want to achieve. Without a clear purpose it is very easy to become confused in what you are doing. Your purpose for being in the sharemarket drives everything else: you cannot decide on your ends or set your strategies and identify your targets if you do not define your purpose. Knowing your purpose stops you going off into other areas of, or activities on, the sharemarket, stops you being tempted into some 'great investment' that you might have heard about but which really does not suit you. Best of all, it stops you blundering around 'trying to make a bit of money'.

Without a clear purpose it is very easy to become confused in what you are doing.

Generally, there are three main purposes for people to invest in shares:

1. To get income.

2. To grow wealth.

3. To become rich.

Some people may have other purposes, or variations on them, but the great majority of investors will answer to one of these purposes.

Don't ever confuse the three. You can't aim both to get rich and get income to spend; neither can you grow your wealth at the same time as getting income. Decide on your purpose and stick to it. If for any reason you do want to have two purposes, you should split the capital that you have to invest and run two distinct portfolios each with its own purpose and plan. For example, if you had $100,000 to invest in shares and wanted both to get some income to live on and grow your wealth you might split your $100,000 into two portfolios of, say, $50,000 each. You would then do a separate plan for each and have two different portfolios of shares.

Most people will have just one purpose and that will be written down at the top of the page on your plan. As well, it will be imprinted deeply in your brain (with a hot branding iron!). Never forget your purpose for going into the sharemarket – and don't deviate from it. If your life circumstances change and alter your purpose and what you want from the sharemarket, you have to go back to the beginning and redo your plan.

Each of these three purposes is perfectly valid in the sharemarket: you can use shares to get income, you can use them to grow your wealth over time, and some people have used shares to become rich. Each purpose requires different skills, different strategies and different risks. Your purpose will largely be dictated by your age and stage in life, your family situation and circumstances, and by your personality. For example, if you are a 76-year-old retiree, you may want to use shares to augment your income – shares do this well because although there is a bit more risk involved, a well-diversified portfolio of income shares should yield far better dividends than a deposit account or bonds, and give you some degree of growth in both income and capital. This is important because even at age 76 you could be retired for another 15 years or longer and an investment solely in bonds or deposits will see the whittling away over time of the spending power of your income by inflation.

> You cannot do anything properly if you don't know the reason for doing it.

At the other end of the spectrum could be a 28-year-old who has a drive to become rich from shares. If that is you, you may put off buying a house and use all of your capital and spare income to trade and invest in growth shares. You might be aggressive enough to gear up your share portfolio, borrowing and using margin trading facilities or options and warrants. What you do is driven by your purpose. Quite simply, you cannot do anything properly if you don't know the reason for doing it.

E IS FOR ENDS

Your ends have to be very specific and numerical. There can be no waffling about your ends; they are what you want to achieve, where you want to end up, and they have to be expressed in numbers. Because they are expressed in numbers, they are not easy to avoid when you are measuring your success.

Your ends are your specific outcomes. Usually they will be one or more of these:

1. Have a particular amount of money in the market at a certain time.
2. Achieve a certain return or profit.
3. Receive a specific amount of income.

Because the ends have to be set in numbers, they might be something like this:

1. To have $100,000 in the market by the end of the year, $150,000 by the end of the next year, etc.

2. To achieve a total return (income plus capital growth) of 20% p.a.

3. To outperform the NZX50 by 5%.

The difficulty with setting these ends is, of course, that the sharemarket does not produce even returns – it is quite volatile. You may be able to set precisely how much money you will put in the market (from income or savings), but the returns are likely to be lumpy and uneven. While you might want to achieve 20% overall, you will find that one year the market will return 30%, the next year minus 20%, the year after that 40%, etc. The returns only average out over long periods of time. Therefore, do not be panicked by poor returns in any one year or period. Have a look at what you are doing by all means – but if your ends seem reasonable and strategies good, stay with them – patience is the greatest virtue with shares.

This volatile nature of shares is why some people set as one of their ends a return based on their performance compared to the market average. These people set a particular index (e.g. NZX50) as the benchmark, and then try to beat that by a certain amount: say by 5% or 10%. This is a reasonable end: you know that the market will produce good returns over the long term and your job is to beat it by a particular amount. This still will not work out perfectly at all times – the shares that you have chosen which would beat the average may not have gone up at the time that you are measuring your performance. Therefore you may not have beaten the market by the desired amount at the particular year end that you have chosen. There is no point worrying too much about this – as long as you are confident that

> **As long as you are confident that what you are doing is the right thing, stay patient.**

what you are doing is the right thing, stay patient.

Obviously your ends will have been set by your purpose. Someone wanting to get rich from shares will be looking for $2m in the market and/or will be trying to double their money in the market each year. Someone looking to get income from shares will have as ends a dividend return of 9% or to receive $4,500 each year from a $50,000 portfolio. The purpose drives the ends. Once the ends are set you can think about how you are going to achieve them.

S IS FOR STRATEGY

Your strategies fall under four main headings:

1. The types of shares you are going to invest in.
2. How you are going to divide up your capital.
3. Where the money is going to come from.
4. A set of policies that are dictated by the ends you have set yourself.

Providing your ends are realistic, you have to find a way of achieving them. You may find that the strategies you wish to adopt will not achieve those ends. That means that you will either have to have another look at your ends (perhaps you won't be able to achieve a 30% return) or think a bit harder about your strategies. For example, to achieve 30%, you may have to use some gearing techniques (margin trading or use of warrants and options). If gearing is not attractive to you, perhaps a 15% return is more realistic.

TYPES OF SHARES

Shares can be used for growth, for income or for speculation. Sometimes the same share can give you two of these things (for years, Telecom gave both great income and good growth). However, this is unusual and should not be relied on – usually a company will give greater growth than income or vice versa. Other shares are good for trading or speculation, such as those of very low value (penny dreadfuls) or whose share price shows great volatility. According to your ends, you will decide to go into particular types of shares.

DIVIDING YOUR CAPITAL

Most of us are not only looking for growth or wanting income. The majority, regardless of their main purpose, will want to do some stagging or trading. This may in fact suit some investors looking for income. They may decide not to try to get all of that income from dividends, but to get some of it from stagging any IPO that comes along. Similarly, people who want to beat the market index by say 5% or 10% will probably want to do that through stagging or some judicious trading.

Decide on the proportion of your capital that will go into particular types of shares and how much you will keep aside for trading special opportunities. For example, you may decide to put 90% of your capital into good long-term growth shares and hold 10% for stagging or trading. Once you have set this proportion do not go outside it. Trading is risky and you need to resist the temptation of putting more money into that area because a 'special' opportunity has come along. If a special opportunity arises which is very tempting and you already have your full allocation out in trading stock, you will need to find the money for the new opportunity by selling one of your trading shares.

AMOUNT OF CAPITAL TO GO INTO THE MARKET

Clearly this will need to match up with your ends. If one of your ends is to have $50,000 in the market in two years' time, you probably won't achieve that with the $10,000 you have at the moment.

There are two ways that you can meet your end of having a certain amount of money in the market:

1. The capital that you put in.

2. The profits (both dividends and capital growth) that you will retain in the market.

These two together have to add up to your stated end of having a particular amount of money in the market at a certain time.

Of the two of these, your capital input is the most controllable and the easiest to plan. You know the amount of money that you have in the market now, you know how much other money (savings or investments) that you have and wish to commit to the market, and you can take a good guess at how much spare cash from your income you will be able to put into the market. Add these up and that is your input into the market.

Then you have to look at what sort of returns you will get from the market with the money that you have in there. This is obviously much more problematical. As mentioned before, the market is volatile and does not produce steady returns. Even if it did, your capital is not likely to go into shares all at the same time – you will put more cash in as it becomes available. Therefore this area is likely to require a bit of educated guesswork. There is no point in trying to be too precise about it – it will not work out neatly.

However, look at the return that you are hoping for under your ends, look at the time that the various parts of your cash input will go into the market and try to work it out.

For example, a family has stated ends of having $100,000 in the market in two years' time and is looking for returns of 15% p.a. A plan to get that $100,000 might be:

Currently invested in sharemarket	$ 40,000
Savings	$ 20,000
Cash from income ($10,000 p.a.)	$ 20,000
Profits from shares	$ 20,000
	$100,000

The 'profit from shares' is a rough guess, based on getting 15% p.a. and thinking approximately when the money will go in. There is no point in using a sophisticated computer spreadsheet here: the profit will not be exactly 15% nor will the money go in exactly when planned.

There is a whole range of other strategies which are dictated by your ends. If you are not prepared to set a particular strategy to meet certain ends, then you must be prepared to change your ends. For example, if an end was to get a 50% return from the market but you were not prepared to take considerable risk and put in a lot of time, then the end is simply unrealistic. You will have to bring that return down to something achievable, given the amount of risk you are prepared to take. The headings that you will need strategies for are:

- **Gearing.** If your aim is to get rich through shares you will have to borrow: if you are looking for income, forget it! Those in between may choose to use limited gearing techniques, perhaps using warrants or options. If your end is to achieve over 30% p.a. from the market you will have to gear up (or do some very clever trading).

- **Dividends.** If your end is to become rich or grow your wealth, you will certainly want to invest in companies that pay out only a little of their profits or find a way of reinvesting dividends. This may be easy: if you have enough in the market, every time you receive a dividend cheque you buy more shares. Alternatively, you could choose companies which issue shares in lieu of dividends. Perhaps the simplest strategy is to buy into shares which pay out little or none of their profits by way of dividends but retain all of their earnings to grow the company. Obviously, if your purpose is to obtain income from your portfolio, you will look for companies which pay

> **If your purpose is to obtain income from your portfolio, you will look for companies which pay out most of the profit as dividends.**

out most of the profit as dividends, bank the cheques and spend the money.

- **Timing.** To make big profits from shares you will need to try to time the market – buy low and sell high. Those who are less aggressive will simply buy and hold.
- **Risk.** Shares are subject to both types of risk – performance risk (the risk that an investment might collapse in value) and volatility risk (the thrashing around, the ups and downs of the share price performance). You can only receive higher returns from your investments if you are prepared to take risks.
- **Selling**. Establish a policy of either buying good businesses and holding them long term or selling out when a company's share price reflects full value. Theoretically, selling when the share price has risen to full value then putting your money into something else will give the best returns. However, in the real world that is hard to do. Experience teaches us that buying and holding long term gives the best chance of success.

Buying and holding long term gives the best chance of success.

All of these things make up your strategies. Once they are settled and you are certain they will meet your ends, you can look at your targets.

T IS FOR TARGETS

Now that you know the types of shares you want, you should be looking to identify your targets. Note that these are at this stage only targets – they are not the shares that you will necessarily buy. Most experienced investors watch their targets for some time before they place a buy order. They might buy a small number early on, but unless there is some reason to buy urgently it is better to watch what a company is doing, follow its announcements and observe the shorter-term patterns of the share price to try to find a cheap entry point.

Spending this sort of time in observation is not always practical as the market may be waking up to the value that a company represents and start pushing up its share price. However, the longer that you can watch, the better will be your decisions. If a share moves significantly and you miss out, don't beat yourself up too much – there will be other good investments available, there always are. The best sharemarket investors are not impetuous – the whole point of planning is that it removes you from the emotional hurly-burly of the market and helps you to invest with your head, rather than your heart. Thinking (rather than feeling) and patience are what good sharemarket investing is about. It is a science, not an art, and you should go about it clinically.

The best sharemarket investors are not impetuous . . .

To show how this whole planning exercise can work, it is best to look at a real example. This is a couple in their mid-40s who have paid off their mortgage and been investing in shares for several years. Their plan looks like this:

Smith Share Plan Jan 2010

Purpose: To grow wealth

Ends	Strategies	Targets
1. To have $200,000 in shares by Jan 2013	85% in growth shares	**50% Overseas** • WiNZ • Unit trusts (?)
2. To get a 12% return	15% held back for trading	• Standard Chartered Bank (UK) • Platinum Asia Fund

Smith Share Plan Jan 2010 Purpose: To grow wealth		
	Money to come from: In market today $50,000 Family loan due 1.4.12 $60,000 Income ($15,000 p.a.) $45,000 Reinvest profits $50,000 Total 1.1.13 $205,000	**50% NZ** • GPG • NZ Oil and Gas • Michael Hill • Infratil • Pumpkin Patch • Ryman Healthcare • Goodman Property Trust
	Policies • Medium risk • No gearing • Reinvest all dividends • Hold good businesses long term	**Trading (NZ only)** • Take up all IPOs • No more than 2 penny dreadfuls • Special situations/ takeovers

PLANNING EXAMPLE

Most of this plan is fairly self-explanatory. The point is that this family has a plan which they would have spent no more than an hour or two writing and, more importantly, which is short and easy to understand. Certainly they will have more work to do as they investigate further the targets that they have identified. In fact these workings, notes and calculation of P:Es, nta, dividend yield and profit growth are likely to involve a great deal of detailed work.

The point of the plan, however, is that the right targets are identified. The plan itself won't tell you specifically which shares to buy, but it will put you in the right area. You won't waste your time analysing the wrong stuff nor waste your money buying it.

It seems to me that to avoid these pitfalls, it is certainly worth spending an hour or two sketching out a plan!

PART 3

The language of the market

Glossary

Abnormal item
A transaction that does not usually happen in a company, is unlikely to recur and which has been especially large.

Accrual rules
Accounting rules which adjust a company's accounts so that items are accounted for when income or expenditure is incurred or committed, rather than when cash changes hands.

Amortisation
When a company systematically reduces the value of an asset in its books.

Arbitrage
Taking advantage of a price difference between the market for an asset and the derivatives (or futures) market of the same asset; or a price difference between two markets (e.g. Australian Stock Exchange and New Zealand Stock Exchange). Arbitraging entails buying in one market and simultaneously selling in the other to make a profit.

Asset stripping
Buying a company below its asset value and then breaking up the company and selling it off to make a profit.

Audit
An independent checking and verifying of the company's accounts; the auditor confirms that the accounts are a fair view of the company's finances. All companies that are listed on the stock exchange must have their accounts audited.

Bear
A pessimist who believes the market will fall.

Bid
An offer to buy at a price.

Blue chip
A big company that is well established and therefore regarded as very safe and secure.

Bonus issue
Where shares are issued free to shareholders. Shareholders are not necessarily any better off, because the extra shares dilute the assets and earnings per share accordingly.

Bottom up
The approach to investment which looks first at the individual company, then at the industry that it trades in, and finally the economy that it is a part of (c.f. *top down*).

Bourse
French for stock exchange. The original bourse was in Belgium and closed in 1998 after 500 years of trading.

Bull
An optimist who believes the market will rise.

Call option
The holder has the right to buy a share at an agreed price on a certain date.

Capital index
Measures only the change in price of the shares and ignores dividends.

Capital note
A fixed-interest investment. An investor lends money to a company without security and receives a fixed rate of interest.

Cash box
A company that has lots of cash as its main asset. This is usually a company that has sold its assets or business and now has a lot of cash, which it might either give back to shareholders or use to acquire other businesses.

Cash issue
An issue of shares for cash by a company to its exisiting shareholders in proportion to their shareholding.

Charting
Trying to predict the future direction of a market by studying charts and graphs.

Conglomerate
A company with business divisions in a wide range of different industries.

Contract note
A note sent by a broker confirming the sale or purchase of shares.

Contributing shares
Shares where only part of the value is paid up and the holder has an obligation to pay the balance in the future. Also called *partly paid shares*.

Convertible shares
Shares that can be converted to ordinary shares.

Cum dividend
With the dividend – shares which are cum dividend carry the right to an upcoming dividend.

Current asset
An asset that can be readily turned into cash, such as stock or accounts receivable.

Current liability
A liability that must be paid within one year.

Debenture
An instrument which secures money lent to a company by giving the lender first charge over the company's assets.

De-listing
The process of withdrawing a company from having its shares traded on the stock exchange – may be temporary or may be permanent.

Diluted capital
The shares that a company has on issue may be diluted by partly paid shares or options, meaning that when these new shares are issued from the options or partly paid shares there will be a greater number of shares on issue.

Dividend cover
The number of times that a company's dividend is covered by its profits. For example, if a company paid out one third of its profits in dividends, it would have a dividend cover of 3.

Don't sell notice
A notice that companies are required to make to the stock exchange when something happens which might affect the value of the shares. It often means that a takeover or some major acquisition or disposal is happening.

Dual listing
When a company is listed on two stock exchanges (e.g. New Zealand and USA).

Earnings
The profits of a company, usually tax paid.

Earnings per share (eps)
The amount of earnings (or profit) attributable to each share. Calculated by dividing the earnings by the number of shares on issue.

$$\text{eps} = \frac{\text{earnings}}{\text{shares on issue}}$$

Earnings yield
The yield that an investor would receive if all of the company's profit was paid out. This is the inverse of the P:E ratio but expressed as a percentage. For example, a company on a P:E of 20 would have an earnings yield of 5%.

Elliott Wave theory
A form of charting (or technical analysis) which says that markets rise in five major waves and then fall in three waves.

Entitlement
An issue of shares which an existing shareholder is entitled to buy (see *Cash issue*).

Equities
Another word for shares – it represents ownership of a business or company as opposed to lending it money.

Ex dividend
Without the dividend – shares go ex dividend and therefore do not carry the right to the dividend payment.

Extraordinaries
Transactions which are outside a company's usual course of business.

FASTER
New Zealand's screen-based trading system (Fully Automated Screen Trading and Electronic Registration).

Final dividend
Companies often make two dividend payments, the interim dividend and the final dividend. Adding the two together gives the annual dividend payout and this figure is used to calculate the dividend yield.

Float
A company offering its shares for sale, usually listing on the sharemarket at the same time.

Fully paid shares
Shares in a company on which no further payment is due. These contrast with *partly paid shares, instalment receipts* and *contributing shares* where another payment must be made.

Fundamentalist
One who makes investment decisions on the basis of the fundamentals of a company and its finances.

Gearing
Borrowing to buy an income-earning asset.

Gross index
An index which includes dividends being added to its value and therefore measures the gross returns (capital and dividends).

Gross yield
The dividend yield before tax.

Hedging
Using synthetics or derivatives to offset a possible loss.

Imputation credit
A credit attached to a dividend reflecting the fact that the company has already paid tax on its profits.

Index
The measure of the way a market changes over time. Sharemarket indices are the value of a basket of defined shares. As the value of the shares changes, so too does the index.

Index funds
A managed fund which simply tracks an index – e.g. TENZ or WiNZ.

Instalment receipts
Shares that are issued after two or more payments are received. For example, the first payment is made and the instalment receipt is listed on the market, but there is an obligation to make the other payment in, say, two years' time.

Interim dividend
The dividend that is paid mid-year. It is usually smaller than the *final dividend*.

Limit order
An order to a sharebroker, limiting the price at which the broker can buy or sell.

Liquidation
The sale of assets and the termination of the company.

Listed trust
Managed funds where the units of the trust are listed on the stock exchange.

Margin
The deposit paid by an investor who is borrowing to buy shares or futures contracts.

Market capitalisation
The value of all of the company's shares. The market capitalisation would be the amount that you would have to pay to buy the entire company at its current share price.

Net
An amount after all deductions.

Net tangible assets
The value of the company's tangible assets after deduction of any liabilities. Note that tangible assets are things that you can touch and therefore do not include things like goodwill, the value of brands or trademarks, etc.

Net yield
The dividend yield after tax.

New Zealand Stock Exchange
Owned by sharebrokers, the NZX accepts shares for quotation by its members and effectively makes the market for the buying and selling of shares.

No liability
Companies where the holders of partly paid shares have no liability (or obligation) to pay further calls.

Odd lot
A small parcel of shares (usually less than 100).

Offer
A quote to sell a share.

Off market
The sale of shares not made on the stock exchange but arranged privately.

Ordinary shares
Shares which have been fully paid up, which have voting rights and rights to dividends and to capital on winding up.

Overbought
A situation where a share seems to be highly priced – too many people have bought it.

Overhang
A situation where there are a large number of shares for sale, overhanging the market and depressing the price.

Oversold
A situation where a share seems too cheap – too many people have sold it.

Oversubscribed
A float of shares where demand from investors exceeds the number of shares available.

Paper profits
Profits brought about by the appreciation in value of an asset but which have not been realised (made real) by selling. Some would say that there is no such thing as a paper profit – no profit is made until the cash has been banked.

Pari passu
Equal – a security that ranks 'pari passu' ranks equally in terms of the rights to vote or receive dividends.

Partly paid shares
See *Contributing shares*.

Penny dreadful
A share which trades for just a few cents. Highly speculative, they seldom have any earnings but can be good for traders because of the large percentages involved in an apparently small change in value.

P:E ratio
The most important ratio for valuing businesses and shares, the price:earnings ratio compares the earnings (or profit) from a share with the price to be paid. Calculating the P:E ratio is a two-step process:

1. Calculate the earnings for each share (earnings per share) by dividing the company's tax-paid profit by the number of shares on issue

$$\text{earnings per share} = \frac{\text{profit}}{\text{shares on issue}}$$

2. The P:E ratio is then calculated by dividing the share price by the earnings per share

$$\text{P:E ratio} = \frac{\text{share price}}{\text{eps}}$$

The best companies have very high P:E ratios – their prices are high compared to their earnings because those earnings are sustainable and growing. Most investors look for companies that are selling on P:E ratios that are lower than are warranted and wait for the market to rate the company more appropriately.

PEG
Price earnings ratio compared to growth of a company's earnings. Generally a PEG of less than one is considered desirable – i.e. the percentage growth in a company's earnings is greater than its P:E ratio. However, there are a lot of exceptions to this.

Preference shares
Shares which in the event of liquidation would see the holders paid in preference to the ordinary shareholders.

Profit taking
Realising profits after a good run. Usually results in a 'technical correction' – i.e. a short-term down trend.

Proxy
The person to whom you give the right to vote at a shareholders' meeting.

Put option
The holder has the right to sell a share at an agreed price on a certain date.

Quote
An offer or a bid – i.e. an asking price to sell, or an offer to buy.

Reverse takeover
A takeover of one company by another where the buying company intends to place its business assets into the takeover target.

Scrip
Share certificates, largely a thing of the past, with scripless trading operating in most countries around the world.

Bibliography

Balmer, Duncan, *The Investment Jungle*, (HarperCollins 1998), NZ

Buffett, Mary and Clark, David, *Buffettology*, (Fireside 1997), USA

Chignell, Agnes, *Company Basics – Running a Company in New Zealand*, (Toha Kape Ltd 1997), NZ

Donnelly, Austin, *Sensible Share Investing*, (Wrightbooks 1996), Aust

Jamieson, Bill, *Bemused Investor's Guide to Company Accounts*, (Shoal Bay Press 1998), NZ

Kerr, George and Hin, Aaron, *Safe Haven – Value Investing – A Certain Strategy for an Uncertain World*, (Penguin 1999), NZ

Koch, Richard, *Selecting Shares that Perform*, (Financial Times 2000), UK

Lowe, Janet, *Value Investing Made Easy*, (McGraw-Hill 1996), USA

Lowe, Janet, *Warren Buffett Speaks*, (John Wiley & Sons 1997), USA

McCarter, Nigel, *Shorten the Odds*, (The Dunmore Press 1997), NZ

Maller, Valerie F. and Kaye, Stuart P., *How to be a Growth Investor*, (McGraw-Hill 1999), USA

Newman, Frank with Briggs, Phil, *Making Money on the New Zealand Sharemarket*, (Dollars and Sense Books 1999), NZ

The New Zealand Company Register, (Mercantile Gazette Marketing – annual), NZ

New Zealand Investment Year Book, (Datex – annual), NZ

The Share Investor's Handbook, (Information Australia 2000), Aust

Index